NEW RULES FOR OPERATIONS PORTFOLIO MANAGEMENT

BUILDING YOUR BUSINESS FUTURE

LARRY TU, WARRIOR AND AUTHOR

TABLE OF CONTENTS

Table of Contents

TABLE OF DIAGRAMS

TABLE OF CHART & GRAPHS

TABLE OF TABLES

WHY I WROTE THIS BOOK
FOR YOU

The concepts of innovation are very popular topics these days. Are they something only people like Elon Musk or Steve Jobs can do? What do they mean to us?

I wrote this book over the past several months in the morning and weekends, because I wanted to help all those who dream of wild ideas and disruption concepts bring them into reality. I want to help you be one of those entrepreneurs who not only dreams wild ideas and disruption concept, but also gets these ideas into reality.

I'm not talking about academic book learning, nor am I talking about the information or data you can get from the internet. I'm talking about real world experiences and examples that would help you to run your business with more consistency and efficiency, focusing on real results.

When we have many ideas floating around, we got to have a systematic way to manage many aspects of business. For an organization's success, product branding, market campaigns, sharing of best practices are all considered to be contributing factors.

Within an organization, we need to:

- Get everyone on the same page about what we need to accomplish,
- Determine what are most important things we need to focus,
- Consider whom we have to rely on to get the solution developed, and
- Be aware of our commitments and their development as well.

We live with purpose and we exist for others. We find our happiness when we keep our purpose with fulfillment.

I want to help business entrepreneurs to grow in their knowledge and build the successful business of their dreams.

I hope I've succeeded in some small way. I'm fulfilled when I see you grow and achieve your goals as a result of my book.

A LITTLE ABOUT ME

I am an executive achieving real results by balancing the art and science of operations management.

I have worked as an entrepreneur as well as an executive in large global corporations.

Working at those big companies was a great way to prepare me to build and manage several of my own businesses.

I have had the opportunities to manage large cross-disciplinary global teams, consolidating operations of merged companies into an integrated model critical to and aligned with corporate strategic plans.

With an entrepreneurial track record of leveraging product deployment combined with operations management skills, I have launched multiple successful businesses.

I have a wonderful family with two grown up kids, and have spent most of my time in Silicon Valley over the past 25 years.

HOW TO START BENEFITING RIGHT AWAY

For basic concept, you may read the chapter of "What is Operations Portfolio Management (OPM)".

To understand the latest trends, you may read the chapter of "New Rules for Today's OPM".

To avoid common mistakes, you may go through "OPM Do's and Don'ts".

Sections of "OPM Tricks/Tips", "Secrets Executives Need to Know" and "Myths and Misconceptions" provide you with additional tips and clarifications.

For implementing Operations Portfolio Management, you may refer to "SPOT for Operations Portfolio Management (OPM)".

"OPM Fundamentals" gives you all details you need to know about Operations Portfolio Management.

You may refer to Real World Case Study at the end to learn my real world experiences.

WHAT IS OPERATIONS PORTFOLIO MANAGEMENT (OPM)?

Portfolio management is usually linked with financial strategies. You manage the risk and investment return in the portfolio by adjusting the mix and amount of different investments. Usually, they won't rise or fall to the same degree or simultaneously.

Instead of putting all of your money in one place, you spread it around and create a diverse portfolio of different types of investments such as stocks, bonds, small-cap, large-cap, domestic, international, and etc.

Similarly, this thought process can also be applied to organization's strategy delivery including Innovation.

Companies that continually innovate don't put all their eggs in one basket. Instead they create portfolios of innovation projects of different types, technologies, and markets, with large numbers of early stage projects and smaller numbers over time.

The companies then actively manage these portfolios by allocating resources differentially, and periodically killing some projects while doubling down on others.

Quite often, companies struggle with bringing successful innovation to market because they don't manage the portfolio of innovations with enough discipline. They let poorly performing efforts continue while not investing in other products with more potential.

Operations Portfolio includes aligned and prioritized activities of all spending and resources on delivering an organization's strategic objectives. It covers Innovation, New products, Investments, Capital, Asset management, Services, Merger & acquisitions, Compliance, and IT Projects.

Operations Portfolio Management is the integrated management of one or more portfolios, and it includes identifying, prioritizing, managing, and controlling projects, programs, services and other related work in order to obtain specific strategic business objectives of the organization as a whole.

- If an organization does not have any programs but has only individual projects, all these projects can be grouped into one or more portfolios.
- If an organization has programs and no individual project external to all programs, all these programs can be grouped into one or more portfolios.
- If an organization has some services, some programs and some individual projects, all these services, programs and projects can be grouped into one or more portfolios.

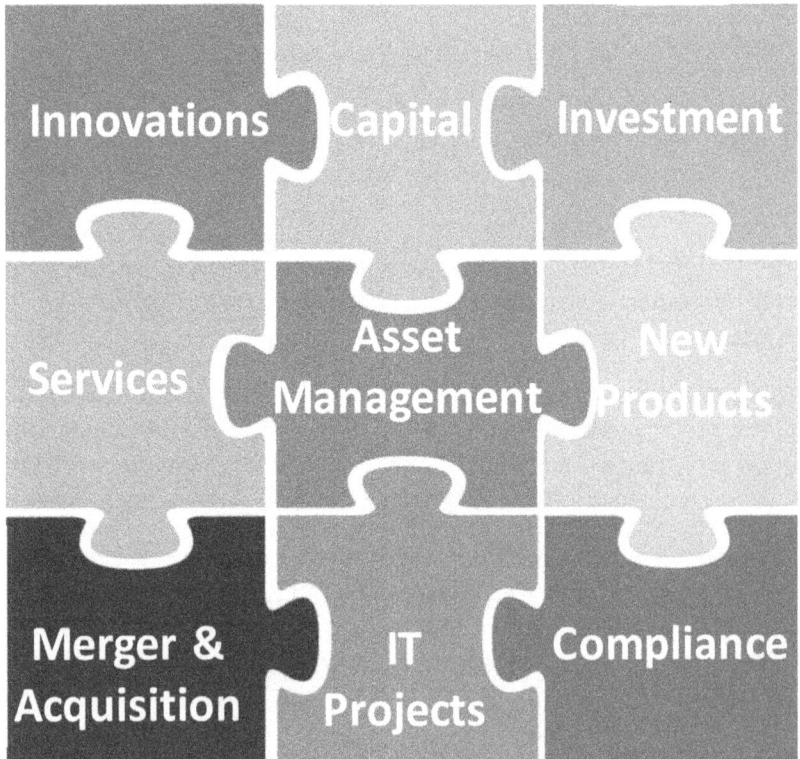

>> *Diagram Operations Portfolio* <<

14

So the structure consists of:

1. A Project Manager manages the activities required to keep the project in control and accomplish the project objectives within defined levels of tolerances,

2. A Program Manager oversees the grouped projects and coordinates efforts between them and

3. A Portfolio Manager is accountable for the success of the whole strategy put forth by the organization.

Program Management focuses on achieving the benefits that would be aligned with the portfolio and hence with the strategic objectives of the organization. So, a portfolio is part of the interface between the programs and strategic business objectives of the organization for which the programs are run.

Operations Portfolio Management (OPM) focuses on making sure that programs and services are prioritized to ensure allocation for resources to serve the organization's strategy. In simpler terms, a portfolio manager worries about the success of the whole strategy put forth by the organization rather than the success of a single project. Therefore, investment decisions are usually made at the portfolio level.

OPM transforms organization's vision and mission into a practical plan. It drives an organization to establish and implement the portfolio, and to manage projects and programs within the portfolio efficiently.

OPM focuses on the execution of the innovation strategy.

There are many elements in execution management such as implementation lifecycle, project management and governance. OPM integrates everything to ensure that all execution activities are fully aligned with the strategic objectives.

OPM enables a better management of interdependencies and resource balance across projects. Every business function, globally or locally, that is involved in multiple projects has to allocate their resources to meet their delivery commitments.

OPM allows an integrated planning and tactical resource allocation, balancing available skills satisfying these project requirements.

Furthermore, OPM enables the coordination of interdependencies across on-going and upcoming projects, maximizing efficiency across the entire portfolio.

Different functions will be involved in projects at different times. For example, it will be unusual for Research and Marketing to have the same intensity of activities on one project throughout its execution.

OPM allows individual business functions to plan the activities for which they are responsible, allocate their resources appropriately, and deliver on their commitments.

While each business function develops their own plans, they should be careful not to establish divergent project portfolios.

The Operations Portfolio Management Manager must ensure not only delivery of the projects and services, but also efficient use of resource during execution.

WHAT MAKES OPM CRITICAL TO YOUR COMPANY

Challenges Businesses with Innovative/ Disruptive Technologies Face

- Doing a lot of things at the same time
- Competing on scarce resources
- Overlapping delivery timelines
- Not everyone is on the same page
- Projects are getting delayed
- People are tied up with tactic activities
- Lack of clear strategic direction
- Poor alignment between goals and projects
- Poor planning and control of action implementation

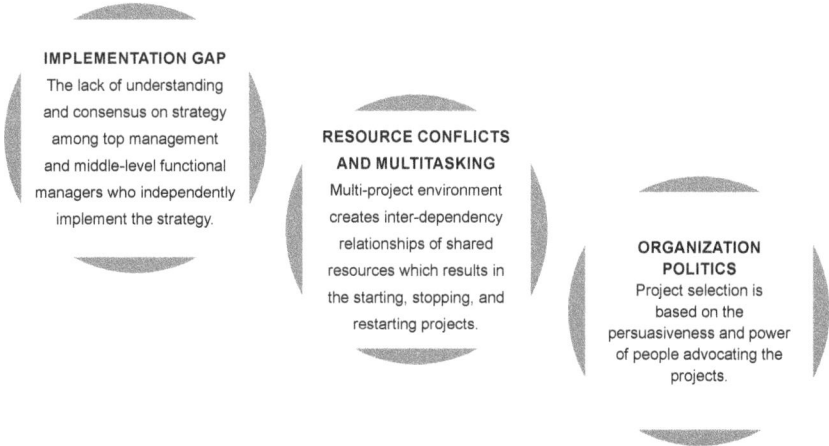

IMPLEMENTATION GAP
The lack of understanding and consensus on strategy among top management and middle-level functional managers who independently implement the strategy.

RESOURCE CONFLICTS AND MULTITASKING
Multi-project environment creates inter-dependency relationships of shared resources which results in the starting, stopping, and restarting projects.

ORGANIZATION POLITICS
Project selection is based on the persuasiveness and power of people advocating the projects.

>> *Diagram Business Challenges* <<

In today's real world business environment, many companies struggle to ensure the realization of the portfolio in an efficient way. For example, they may be doing a lot of things at the same time and often competing the same resource and also overlapping the delivery timeline.

At the end of the day, we were not able to get result we expected. We have to take a pause, assess existing processes, and prioritize our activities to get much better results in a consistent and structured approach.

Another challenge is collaboration among different people and groups. In order to get a job done, it must involve the collaboration and involvement of many functions across the organization. It is not easy to manage different groups, different locations and different time zones. In order to get this done, we need an organized and structured approach.

One more challenge is that many executives are very optimistic which can translate to being aggressive in putting more projects on the list than the organization can accomplish. Most of us tend to think we can do more than what we can.

We can do anything, but we can't do everything.

Not all of us realize:

- the constraint of what the organization has, combined with
- the kind of resource we have

We have to make hard decisions on:

- what kind of things that we can do,
- what kind of things we cannot do,
- and the priorities of what we can and want to do

We have to recognize the dynamics of business in the world today:

Things are changing rapidly.

For example, we work on a project with a lot of resources tied into. If the business conditions change, priorities must change. These resources must be reassigned and reallocated to different priorities.

We have to be able to adjust the project priority, scope, timeline and resources, in order to fit into the challenging and/or changing environment.

Major issues are usually caused by inappropriate management of resources, evidenced by contention amongst team members, improper utilization and no clear matching of capacity to demand.

Leaders must gain a better understanding of practical ways to maximize resources, minimize lost productivity and realize the benefits and results they seek.

Matching Supply to Demand

Another problem an organization often face is that of Matching Supply to Demand.

Too much resource assigned to the project results in wastage, while too little causes frustration for the business and a headache for project manager and team.

For example, in the network area, there might be a limited number of highly skilled network engineers who are specialized in doing the work on the project. All of them are already fully loaded. In this case, demand exceeding supply can arise when we haven't prioritized the new projects yet. We want these engineers to work on those projects right away. Obviously, they just cannot do it because they are already at their full capacity.

The result is that the new projects have to be pushed out or ongoing projects must be delayed.

It's like we have a thousand parts, and the critical path is always on those one or two parts that are in short supply.

If we overloaded those critical resources because we haven't matched their capacity to desired project completion, these critical resources often end up working on many small projects and not the big breakthrough projects.

Although the company is often working on many projects, are they right ones? OPM will answer that question and help you get the critical projects on track to completion.

Growing complexity, accelerating pace, and increasing demands are creating a capacity issue for our existing resources.

Another Challenge is making investment decisions by relying largely on financial approaches.

Investment decisions are often determined using financial approaches such as ROI and Payback period. These methods are fine and certainly appropriate for traditional projects.

The downside of these financial approaches is that they tend to favor incremental projects and put projects on "hold" unless they are what the financial analysis has categorized as sure bets.

Strategic Resources

Failure to set aside strategic resources is quite common for many organizations.

This often results in the organization failing to set aside the strategic resources to undertake these major initiatives and breakthrough projects.

The following guidelines will help leadership make resource allocation decisions and advance the organization.

- Avoid peanut butter spreading or over staffing
- Align and adopt a limited number of prioritization criteria
- Challenge the resource needs and assess alternatives
- Find the critical path

Please review the Strategic Resource Allocation section for more details.

The bottom line is that Resource Management must be part of the overall Operations Portfolio Management governance.

Otherwise, after the Portfolio Prioritization, necessary resources may already be committed to other projects, leaving few or no resources available to do the strategic initiatives. This is often how important projects get postponed or delayed past the time they would be viable.

Boosting Innovation with Operations Portfolio Management

The term of "**Innovation**" is widely used in business world.

Let's talk about what we mean when we talk about "Innovation".

What is Innovation? Does Innovation equate to Ideas?

Many people think innovation is about ideas. Actually, innovation is not just ideas. It is ideas that are acted on, and result in something achieved. Innovation happens as you get things done after a decision has been made.

In my view, idea is 1% of Innovation and execution is 99%.

Innovation is not the same as Ideas. Innovation is Idea plus Execution.

Another misunderstood term: "**Execution**".

Some people think execution is getting a project done based on business scope, target schedule and committed resources. In fact, to realize a great innovation, execution is not just about a project delivery.

The solution for addressing these challenges is Operations Portfolio Management (OPM).

Execution is about using Operations Portfolio Management (OPM) to deliver on Strategy.

Innovation is made possible by the connection of strategy, process, structure, and capability.

Execution is the multiplier of innovation, meaning that an organization that can execute well on a few good innovations is more powerful than one that has lots of great ideas with no way to execute.

Execution does not mean *Delivering a Project*. Rather, Execution is about Operations Portfolio Management (OPM) *Delivering on Strategy*.

WHAT MAKES OPM ESSENTIAL FOR INNOVATIONS?

There are many **benefits** of adopting an organizational wide OPM strategy.

- Streamlined decision making by establishing a collaborative prioritization framework.
- Control risks at individual project level as well as Portfolio level to minimize business impact.
- Optimizing resources with better control and utilization.
- Provide visibility and value to all organization's stakeholders.
- Ensure the continuous improvements on the performance of Operations Portfolio Management.

Streamlined Decision Making

- The leadership has the visibility of project execution performance from a strategic top-down view as well as bottoms-up tactic view.
- They are also able to predict future performance based on past project metrics including scheduling and resource utilization.
- It also exposes projects are not directly contributing to organization's priority and objectives. The leadership can reprioritization ongoing initiatives and reallocate critical resources as necessary.
- It also helps the management to understand how changes on one project impacts the delivery of other projects.
- It also allows the leadership to evaluate multiple scenarios to ensure approved projects will help achieve objectives.

Better Risk Control

There are a number of different kinds of risks, ranging from resources, financial, governance, and mismanaged efforts.

With OPM, management can calculate project benefits, while also being able to identify projects not contributing to organization's objectives.

OPM also supports leadership in efforts to engage and assign accountabilities from responsible functions to ensure the right level of compliance is followed during the project execution.

Optimized Resource Utilization

- A standardized approach allows management to have better visibility on resource utilization.

- It allows the reduction of duplicated efforts, reduce the overall project cost.

- It also allows projects to adopt infrastructure standard with reduced the overall cost of hardware procurement and ongoing maintenance.

- During project peak demand periods, the management can see the overall and specific project demand and redeploy resources accordingly.

- Lastly, it provides the visibility to management to address resources shortages much earlier.

Better Visibility and Better Value to Stakeholders

OPM ensures all stakeholders to have access to the project status and results, giving them a higher comfort level in terms of project prioritization and execution progress.

Also, stakeholders have access to multiple forms of information, including the executive level summary, as well as prioritization status and detailed project status. Executives, business managers and project managers all have access to consistent project execution data from a single source of "truth."

Establishing a Framework for Continuous Improvements

OPM provides a process framework and technology infrastructure that allows organization to continuously execute and deliver on strategies.

ment

It provides repeatable and consistent project execution and success, based on established best practices, combined with a knowledge base and templates to be used within the organization.

With lessons learned and accumulated experiences, future project operations will be improved and benefitted.

Supported by an appropriately structured OPM, organizations can transition from reactive to proactive.

With OPM, we will be able to,

- Maximize the return on investment such as R&D, Manufacturing Capacity and Marketing campaign
- Optimize the utilization of scarce resources
- Tighten the relationship between corporate strategy and project & service selection
- Focus on prioritized projects and activities
- Keep the right balance between short term and long term, high risk and low risk projects
- Provide the transparency on priorities within the organization
- Standardize the project selection process

Please see refer to "SPOT for Operations Portfolio Management" for additional details.

HOW OPM MUST BE UPDATED FOR THE WORLD TODAY

Developing an Innovation Strategy

The organization has to develop an innovation strategy with clear and quantified strategy and long-term goals with dedicated resources. Research has proven that organizations that have clear objectives are more successful in developing breakthrough innovations. Those companies with more experience of working with breakthrough innovation in a structured way as they had more clear objectives than others.

Also, the more successful organizations had specific target allocations for the resources they expected to dedicate.

There are challenges to sustaining commitment for breakthrough projects versus short term projects. It is not easy to handle the challenges for conflict among short term and long term needs.

It is very important to set clear goals and understand upcoming challenge. The organization has to set out a consistent plan with dedicated resources, especially for the coming key stages of a program.

The common challenges are:

- Inability to commit to the long term goals.
- Short-term day to day operations distract and compromise long term breakthrough efforts.

To ensure single-point accountability and commitment at top management levels, the organization must employ a governance approach that ensures long-term accountability and commitment. A dedicated project team is a most effective way to achieve that critical governance.

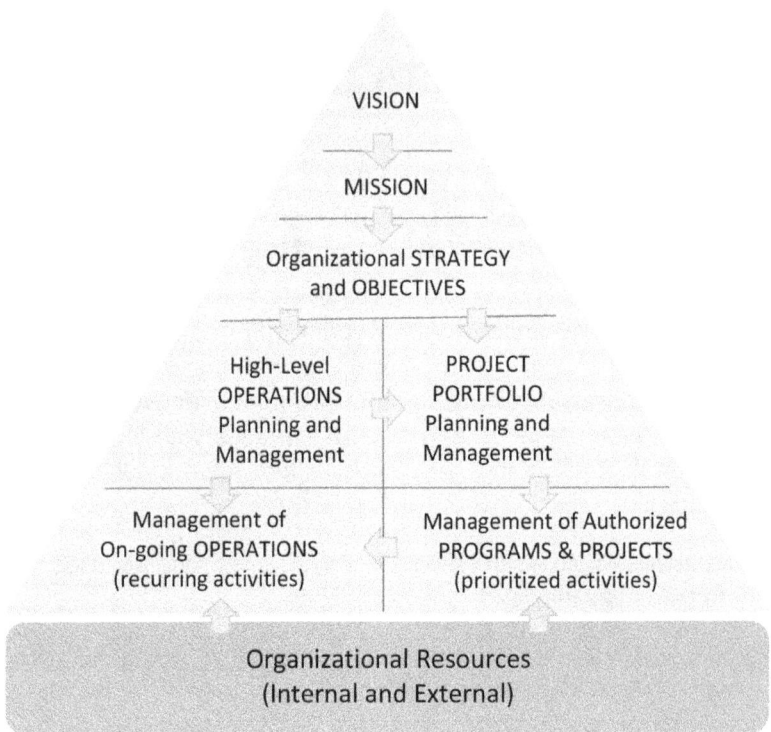

```
                        VISILON

                        MISSION

              Organizational STRATEGY
                  and OBJECTIVES

        High-Level          PROJECT
        OPERATIONS          PORTFOLIO
        Planning and        Planning and
        Management          Management

      Management of         Management of Authorized
    On-going OPERATIONS      PROGRAMS & PROJECTS
    (recurring activities)   (prioritized activities)
```

Organizational Resources
(Internal and External)

>> Diagram Innovation Strategy <<

The Path to Successful Innovation

begins with the following strategic principles.

- Pursue outrageous objectives. Outrageous goals force us to consider alternative processes and technology platforms and thus foster breakthrough innovations.

- Focus on the future.

- Place primary emphasis on customer knowledge and relationships, and secondary emphasis on cost reduction.

- Emphasize process innovation over improvement of existing activities.

- Use advanced technology to drive operating excellence.

- Focus on a few critical core initiatives that span the entire enterprise.
- Use human resources in new, creative ways with structured empowerment.
- Identify and exploit new growth opportunities exposed by breakthroughs.

The Innovation Ambition Matrix

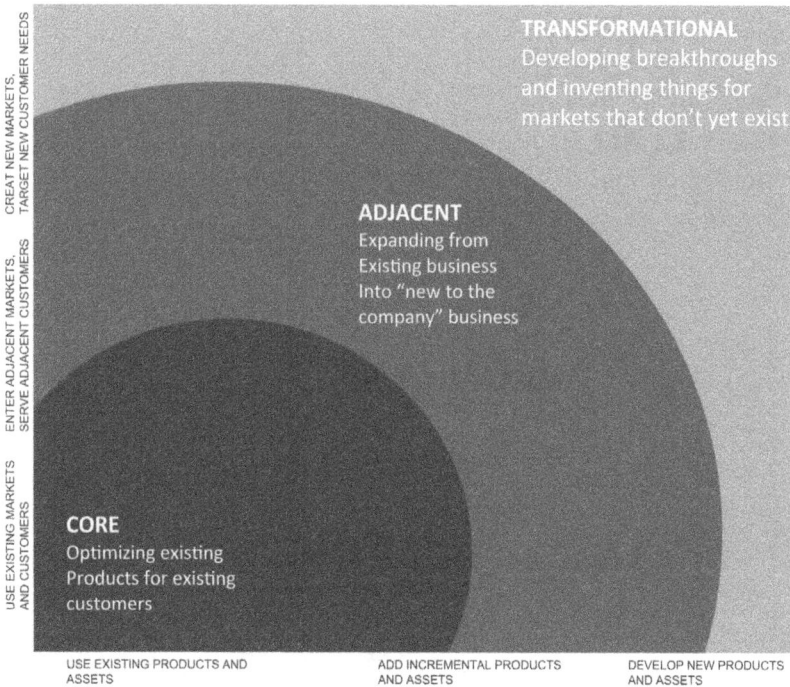

CREAT NEW MARKETS, TARGET NEW CUSTOMER NEEDS

ENTER ADJACENT MARKETS, SERVE ADJACENT CUSTOMERS

USE EXISTING MARKETS AND CUSTOMERS

TRANSFORMATIONAL
Developing breakthroughs and inventing things for markets that don't yet exist

ADJACENT
Expanding from Existing business Into "new to the company" business

CORE
Optimizing existing Products for existing customers

| USE EXISTING PRODUCTS AND ASSETS | ADD INCREMENTAL PRODUCTS AND ASSETS | DEVELOP NEW PRODUCTS AND ASSETS |

>> *Diagram The Innovation Ambition Matrix* <<

Golden Ratio for Resource Allocations

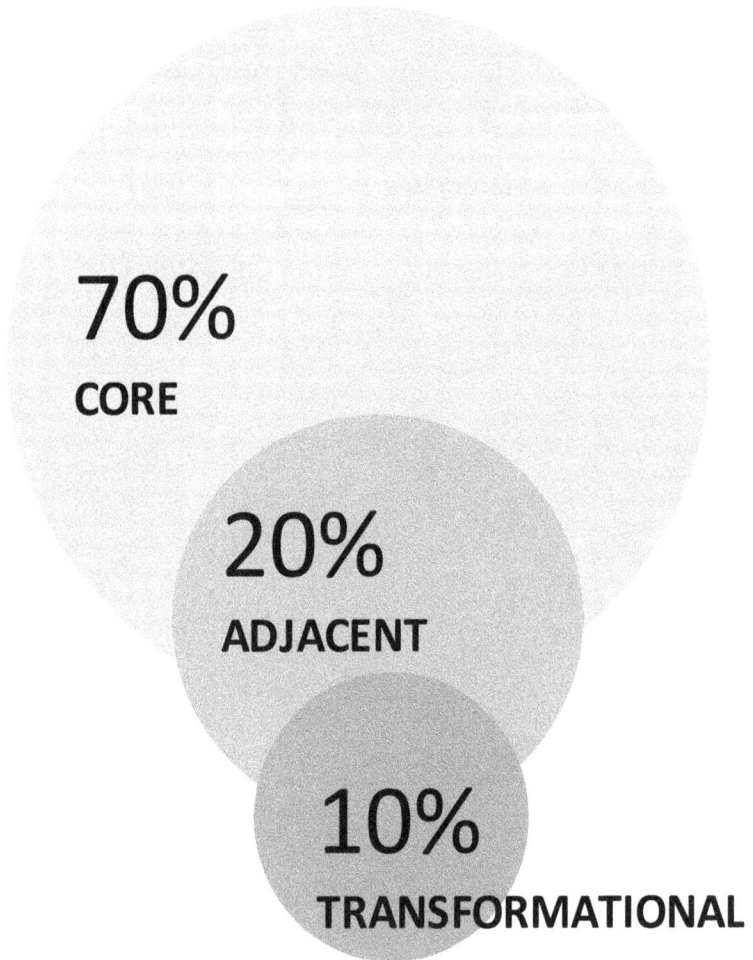

70%
CORE

20%
ADJACENT

10%
TRANSFORMATIONAL

>> *Diagram Golden Ratio for Resource Allocations* <<

Innovation Pays the Bills

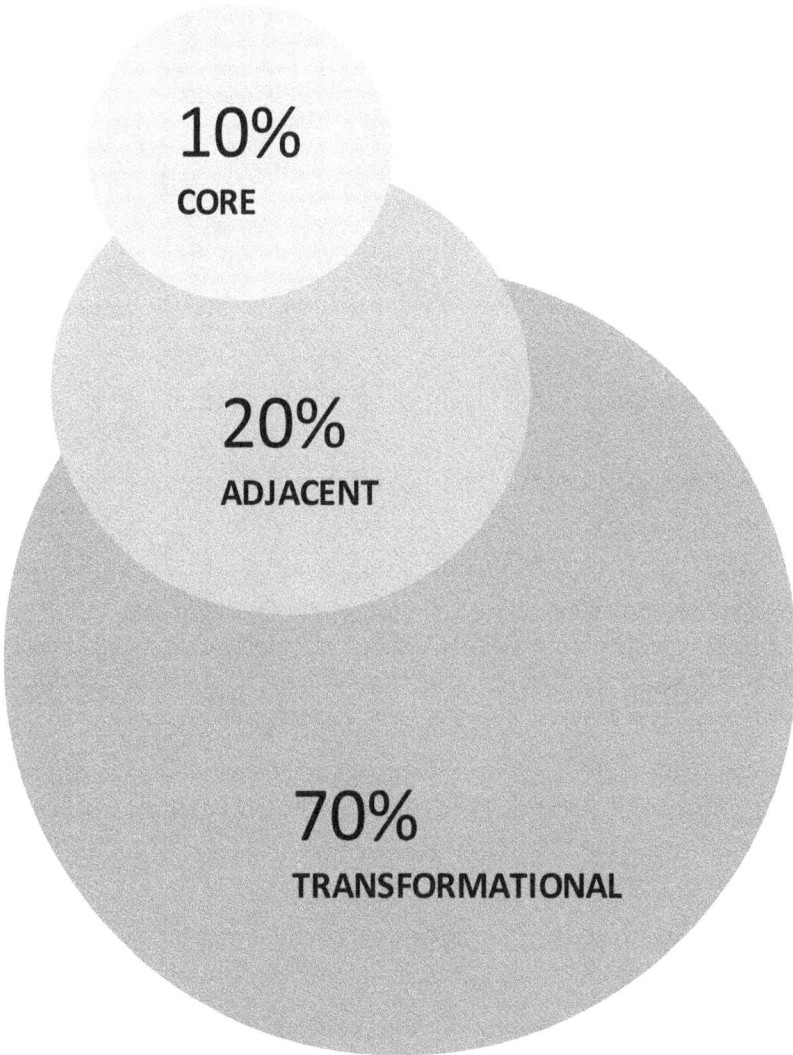

>> *Diagram Innovation Pays the Bills* <<

Different Ambitions, Different Allocations

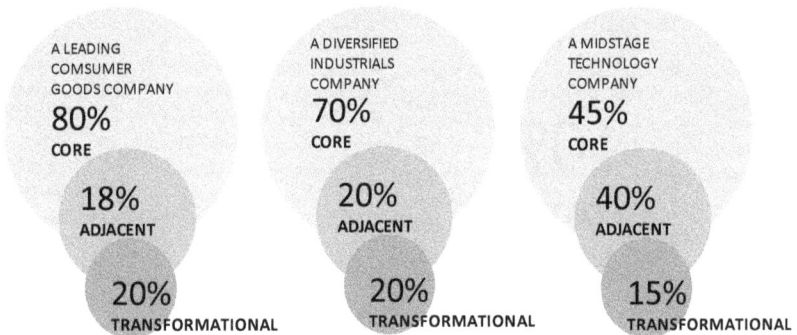

A LEADING
COMSUMER
GOODS COMPANY
80%
CORE

18%
ADJACENT

20%
TRANSFORMATIONAL

A DIVERSIFIED
INDUSTRIALS
COMPANY
70%
CORE

20%
ADJACENT

20%
TRANSFORMATIONAL

A MIDSTAGE
TECHNOLOGY
COMPANY
45%
CORE

40%
ADJACENT

15%
TRANSFORMATIONAL

>> Diagram Different Ambitions, Different Allocations <<

Innovation can be classified into two types as Incremental and Radical, respectively:

Incremental innovation introduces relatively minor changes to the existing product, often applied to existing markets and customers. This type of innovation occurs when companies gain input from customers, who suggest important improvements based on their own product usage and dissatisfaction with current technologies.

On the other hand, radical innovation establishes new sets of core design concepts, and is driven by technological, market, and regulatory forces. The process of radical innovation involves the creation of completely new products,

Your company may have a large number of projects on both incremental and radical innovation competing for scarce resources.

If so, OPM plays a critical role in efficient decisions because it provides the information on which to select the right projects and the right investments at the right time—essential for winning the competition of product innovation. A balanced portfolio with new product and technology is the key for successful product innovation.

How OPM is Different Now

There are many issues with conventional approaches to Operations Portfolio Management.

- Inaccurate or subjective information. Different project managers present data differently, resulting in completely inconsistent formats and widely varying degrees of knowledge across different potential projects. Since project managers also understand that only the highest priority projects will win resources, they may intend to include biased or misleading information to bump up the priority of their projects.

- Lack of consistent prioritization method. The organization's leadership struggles to make consistent decisions that lead to the best company results. It is difficult to decide which project is the top priority.

- Overloaded resources. Without proper planning, resource gap can severely impact the project execution. For example, the organization has limited pool of subject matter engineers required for all projects. It will be very difficult to complete any project until such resource can spend required time on each project.

- Agility. Things change very quickly, and the rate of change continues to accelerate. Traditional Operations Portfolio Management tends to keep the process rigid. This makes it slow and more difficult to respond to constant business changes

How Operations Portfolio Management (OPM) is different now,

Better Tools

- Simplified OPM removes unnecessary components and focus on key areas, Strategize, Prioritize, Optimize and Track. Utilizing standardized tools allows for high efficiency, high transparency and high consistency across all business functions.

Quicker Decision Making

- The business is pushing for shorter decision making cycles. Traditional decisions were in an era where information was either not readily available, or not visible to all stakeholders. In today's

31

world, everything is moving faster with newer technologies. The organization has to bring Operations Portfolio Management up to speed as well.

Multiple perspectives

- Other than these existing processes and approaches, there are new ways of thinking and new tools available for the organization. Leadership can evaluate a wide range of options from the types of projects, to the software tools they can use to determine the business value. With multiple perspectives, leadership can have a broader vision that leads to better strategies.

Adaptive Prioritization Approach

- The organization is focusing on adaptive strategies allowing for quick response for fast changing business environments.

- New messages can move quickly through the system that help the management to respond and make necessary priority adjustment quickly.

OPM DO'S AND DON'TS

DO involve all functions within the organizations in strategy and objective alignment

The entire company leadership should have a clear vision of how the strategy will accomplished. It is critical to collect suggestions and ideas throughout the organization.

If people are not on the same track as the company's goals, take the time to interact with them. Paint the bigger picture, the reason for it, and how you plan to get there.

Don't think of involving all organizations' leadership in the decision making as losing control. On the contrary, involving all leadership members in decision making increased productivity, innovation, and company moral.

Be sure to link your projects to your strategy

If the cascade exercise has been done properly, you should have identified a list of projects and considered their contribution to your strategy at length.

You should also feel satisfied that the project list is correct and that there has been a solid solution to be as creative as possible.

But what if you're not sure?

Draw a simple matrix. Put your strategy themes on one axis and your projects on the other.

Debate assumptions with your executives and don't stop until you all feel that there's a 100 percent fit.

The matrix offers an extra value: it not only helps you to find the white spots or stimulate discussions, but it will also prove to be a great communication tool at a later stage.

Criteria / Weight	Stay within Core Competencies	Strategic Fit	Urgency	25% of sales from new products	Reduce defects to less than 1%	Improve Customer Loyalty	ROI of 18% Plus	Weighted Total
	2.0	3.0	2.0	2.5	1.0	1.0	3.0	
Project 1	1	8	2	6	0	6	5	66
Project 2	3	3	2	0	0	5	1	27
Project 3	9	5	2	0	2	2	5	56
Project 4	3	0	10	0	0	6	0	32
Project 5	1	10	5	10	0	8	9	102
Project 6	6	5	0	2	0	2	7	55
Project n	5	5	7	0	10	10	8	83p

>> Table Link Projects to Strategy Sample <<

DON'T make assumptions

Assumption is the mother of all screw ups.

For example, you assume a key project resource will be available at the time you'd need. Unfortunately, another project he is working on is actually getting delayed, and he has to continue working on that project until it is done. You shall always keep an eye on the status of the dependency project where your key resource is on.

You assume all organizations understand their priority and are fully executing the strategy? Don't assume. Be sure.

DO have a rational and transparent prioritization scheme

Be sure to prioritize all on-going and planned initiatives with a timeline. As the organization place all projects on a common time line horizon, leadership team can determine how much is gained by each project and when the organization will begin to realize the gains.

Here is a sample priority scheme,

A. Mandatory, legal or fix major operational risks

B. Major strategic projects (note that this is not the first on the list)

C. Projects with significant business returns

D. Nice to have

DON'T expect priority and roadmap will stay unchanged

Wouldn't it be easier if you could just draft the organization's portfolio and roadmap once, publish it to the relevant people across the company, and think this is final?

In real world, things change, priorities change and budgets change. Some projects may have seemed so important a few months ago, but with a few changes in your company, maybe not so important in a few months. To navigate potential changes, think of your organization's portfolio and roadmap as reflecting the organization's latest strategic thinking as of now, but not necessarily forever.

You and your Organization will have to make changes throughout the OPM process. There's no way around it. So the more you can think of your portfolio and roadmap as a working, living document — and not a set-in-stone portfolio-roadmap masterpiece, the more success your products will ultimately enjoy in the market.

DO use Tools

Software tools, even in the form of spreadsheets, will help you map out priorities and assignments of all involved teams, track project progress and draw management's attention to possible problems.

Thus, every team can access it from any device. Even better, any updates from any members will be live in real time of Portfolio performance.

All of which makes it possible for senior leadership to have an updated view of the portfolio performance.

DON'T Ignore Risk

The most successful organizations are those who focus on value and getting a consistent result. Over time, these consistent results achieve organization's strategy and objectives, and ultimately are what create big profits.

Of course, long-term perspectives don't provide any short-term rush of achievement, progress, etc.

At the same time, large projects become complex due to new technologies, more regulatory requirements, increased product liability, financing challenges, and the greater dependencies organizations have with multiple business partners. Uncertainty in world markets and government interventions create external risks. These factors can doom an otherwise sound innovation. Many executives know risks in advance. In many cases, however, these risks are mismanaged, misunderstood or unintended.

Risk management enables an organization to limit the negative impact of uncertain events. The risk management process includes Risk Management Planning, Risk Assessment and Risk Mitigation. Please refer to the section of "**Risk Management**" for more details below.

OPM TRICKS/TIPS

Tip: Perform initial project evaluation

Review initial project management tasks like scope, timeline and resource first. Clarify the scope, define deadlines and understand drivers before you set initiative priorities.

Make sure you have a process in place involving experienced project managers who can deliver high-level resource estimates in a short time frame. These carefully considered estimates are essential to selecting the right projects.

The evaluation is done at the start to look at its viability and may be required to be done at several stages of the initiative. An initiative will need to be evaluated to see whether the initiative is on time or needs to be delayed. Will there be any additional costs to the initiative. A Health Check helps in evaluating the initiative based on Scope, Resource and other areas.

>> Diagram Initiative Health Check <<

Tip: Don't try to do everything and be selective

Don't try to do everything because that inevitably means you will end up doing nothing.

Don't try to please every group because that can ultimately hurt the whole company.

Reality shows that an organization can absorb fewer projects than most executives think. Better to hold off until some projects reach the next phase.

Prioritization doesn't mean distributing all available resources to all known projects. Rank your projects and pick the top 30 percent for immediate launch. Put the rest on hold. Repeat the exercise after three-to-six months. The picture will look different as new initiatives arise and projects in process have advanced to different stages.

For example, we may use following prioritization criteria to rank and pick initiatives from all submitted requests.

Prioritization Criteria	SCORE		
	1 point	3 points	5 points
Strategy Delivery	Low 1 objective	Medium 2-3 objectives	High 4 or more objectives
Product Synergies	Low new product with new sales, support and manufacturing	Medium new product with existing sales	High new product with existing sales, support and manufacturing
Profitability	Minor NPV < $1M	Medium $1M < NPV < $5M	Major NPV > $5M
Technical Viability	Very Difficult Major technical obstacles to be resolved	Somewhat Difficult Need to resolve 1 – 3 technical difficulties	Easy No known technical issues
Product Marketability	Low Very few inquires	Medium Several requests of product info	High High interest of the new product
Competition & IP Protection	High Many competitors No IP Protection	Medium 3 – 5 competitors IP Protected	Low 0 – 2 competitors Strong IP Protected
Resources Required	High > 2,000 man-hours, need external resources for more than $100K	Medium 500 - 2,000 man-hours, need external resources between $50K - $100K	Low Less than 500 man-hours and no external resources
Risks	High Regulatory, financial, technical or operational risks	Medium Some regulatory, financial, technical or operational risks	Low Minimum regulatory, financial, technical or operational risks

Tip: You must use a Portfolio Dashboard

Portfolio Dashboard includes,

- Portfolio Status Tracker
- Program/Project Gantt Chart
- Single Page Status Report for each Program/Project
- Risk Register
- Issue Tracker
- Portfolio Budget Tracker

There are several samples for your reference at the section of "Portfolio Level Metrics" below.

SECRETS EXECUTIVES NEED TO KNOW

#1 Secret Executives Need to Know

You will need to constantly adjust and refine the prioritization along with the dynamic of business objectives. The business environment and demand keeps changing. Some initiatives with high priority may be less important, while other initiatives may have higher priority. It is important to be able to adjust the priority to meet dynamic changes in business.

#2 Secret Executives Need to Know

The line between project management and portfolio management is often blurred because people attempt to accomplish all of the tasks we discussed under the heading of project management. For companies that work on a large number of initiatives, it makes sense to clearly delineate between OPM and project management.

To sum it up, OPM focuses on the high-level, strategic decisions for the entire portfolio (doing the right projects), while project management focuses on the execution of individual projects (doing the projects right).

#3 Secret executives need to know

Keep Things Balanced

Start managing your project portfolio by identifying the types of projects that support your business goals. For example, if you have a business plan to become a $100 million a year in a consumer market, you probably won't include many enterprise projects in your plans.

As you start multiple projects, you need to reassess your scoring system. Your scoring system evolves as your business evolves. For example, while you initially might have been focused on projects in the $1 million to $5 million range, if you never reassess you will forever stay working on projects in that range.

You have to adjust the scoring system to account for business growth and the cyclical aspects of the dynamic market. You also have to adjust it to reflect the right mix of projects for your business as you win and complete them. And, because you have included aspects in your scoring system that align with your business' strategic goals, you also need to reassess those aspects as you reach your goals.

Please refer to "**Demand Management**" section for more details on prioritization criteria and process.

MYTHS AND MISCONCEPTIONS

#1 Myth and Misconception
OPM is about Implementing Programs and Projects

Operations Portfolio Management looks at projects and programs in the aggregate, within the context of other programs and the overall connection to **strategy**. These distinctions are especially important to senior leadership.

Management must objectively consider which initiatives are a higher priority based on strategic fit, financial viability, organizational capabilities, and capacity to execute.

#2 Myth and Misconception
OPM is only for Big Companies, Big Investment

Actually, OPM can—and should be-- used by any sizes of companies, small, medium and large. OPM plays an important role in keeping aspects of business organized and structured.

#3 Myth and Misconception
The Best Starting Place is OPM Best Practices

Rarely are companies ready to implement OPM best practices right away. Start first with,

- Standard definitions
- Cost and benefits estimates
- Labor and non-labor estimates
- Stakeholder impacts
- Measureable success criteria
- Return on Investment
- External dependencies
- Stakeholder input

#4 Myth and Misconception
The Right Tool Drives OPM Success

We need to answer following questions before investing any tools,

- Is there an executive commitment to the effort and expense involved?
- Is the rest of the organization prepared for the effort?
- What business benefits must OPM deliver?

The choice of tool is secondary to these considerations. The best tool is the one that most fully serves the very particular needs of the company, regardless of the judgment of the technology marketplace.

NEW RULES FOR TODAY'S OPM

Adapted Prioritization

New technologies emerge to meet various business changing requirements. The Portfolio management must evolve along with technology and business process. The execution plans can be re-prioritized and changed as per demands of situations.

The management must have the courage to cancel or delay projects and programs when that is the right thing to do.

Reviewing results in the context of strategy, the management decides whether a project or program should be cancelled or delayed. For example, a project is no longer aligned to strategy because the changing priorities, focus and expectations. These projects or programs might be executing very well, but they won't deliver the latest strategic results that justify continued investment.

In order to manage the Portfolio with agility, the Portfolio Management has to be an integrated operation, fully aligned with business objectives and strategic goals.

Agile Planning

It is not easy to start a project with all variables and details in a single shot. It is much better to plan and work on phases. It is important to maintain a sense of direction by getting all stakeholders involved in reviews and approvals throughout multiple planning phases.

Agile Planning is different from traditional project planning. It is based on a selection of features that are developed during a specific set of time (the sprint). The ultimate purpose of Agile Planning is to achieve the organization's vision and objectives.

An Agile Plan focuses on planning multiple iterations in an effort to determine when each release will be delivered. In Agile Planning, a project is developed in sprints. The goal of sprint planning is to determine the features and functionality that will be included in the next iteration. Before each sprint begins, a sprint planning meeting takes place between the project owner and development team members. The user stories and backlog are reviewed to determine the tasks that can be completed during the sprint. These plans deliver a finer level of detail (compared to the high-level release plan), including which tasks are to be performed by which team members and how long each task will take.

Activities that occur during the Agile planning process include:

Task Planning: Agile team members break the features down into tasks and then team members take those tasks on. As a matter of best practice, look at the time estimates and try to break any task that may take longer than a day down into smaller tasks. This helps to reduce uncertainty and foster successful task completion. It also feeds into the job of estimating, as it is much easier to estimate the time required to complete a smaller task.

Micro Monitor and Do Not Micro Manage

Traditional project management methodologies are unnecessarily bureaucratic, rigid and tedious for current business environment. These project management requirements often slow down the execution significantly.

Some leaders are too analytical and focus on fine details. They need to understand that the real focus should be on project execution and delivery.

Changes, issues and risks should be monitored, reviewed and addressed with agility. Management's focus should be on project completion, meeting milestones and deliver business requirements.

An effective approach is providing decision makers about the status of Portfolios, Programs, and Projects on a regular base. The management can always have a clear picture on organization's portfolio of strategic initiatives and their performance.

The leadership shall drive and define very clear metrics that are applied in a standardized way cross the organization. Standardization make the decision making less complex and easier to judge.

45

Although Micro Manage has a great involvement and control, it could become a distraction and often causes misuse of resources.

The senior leadership shall pay attention on the things that are important to them. They need to distinguish the awareness vs. interferences. They shall take actions only when needed with the appropriate level of involvement.

More Attention on Risk Management

Establish a centralized repository to track risks of Portfolio, Programs and Projects. It must track all risks with mitigation plans. All stakeholders must not hesitate when it comes to reporting any challenges, concerns and risks. All members should be encouraged to voice their issues and opinions. It leads to fewer surprises, avoiding schedule delay and budget overrun.

Communicate, Communicate and Communicate

The management team must help in creating a picture of deliverables in minds of every person involved in the process. It keeps all stakeholders on the same page by communicating all project activities and deliverables.

Projects are constrained with timeline, resources and budget. It is very importance that all programs and projects must always be led towards completion. It is essential to have periodic updates, follow-ups and meetings.

SPOT FOR OPERATIONS PORTFOLIO MANAGEMENT (OPM)

Steps to Building Operations Portfolio Management Capability

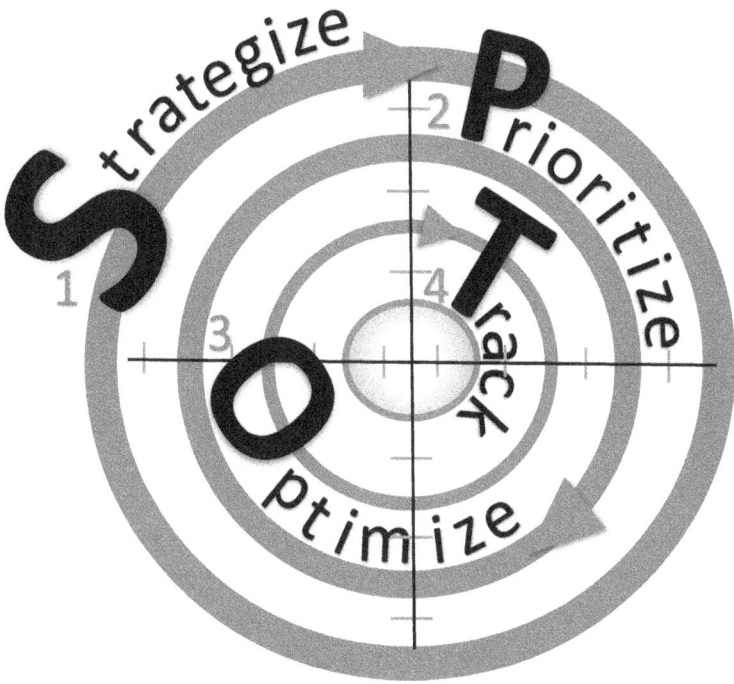

>> SPOT 4-step Diagram <<

SPOT is a 4-step approach to govern and manage organization's Operations Portfolio Management.

SPOT serves as the critical link between executive vision and the execution work. By providing a standard approach for Strategizing, Prioritizing, Optimizing and Tracking from all key activities that comprise today's organization, SPOT gives a coherence to an organization that has long been lacking. SPOT links strategic objectives to individual projects and portfolios.

It will be enlightening and useful for management to take a step back and follow my **SPOT** Operations Portfolio Management approach. It is Strategize, Prioritize, Optimize and Track.

1. Strategize with Alignment & Metrics

Clarify organization's mission and objectives.
Establish a structured management framework.
Define criteria and metrics to measure progress and results.

Align organization's portfolios to advance the company toward its goals. Clearly defined goals for the whole operation.

This includes, for example, mission or vision statements with operational priorities and business targets. Mission and vision statements are a prerequisite for creating value in operations portfolios and projects.

2. Prioritize with Focus & Balance

Collect, evaluate and prioritize all initiatives.

After ensuring alignment, define and select the most promising projects from a value-added point of view. Eliminating projects that aren't aligned reduces waste and optimizes your resource utilization.

3. Optimize with Resource Utilization and Dependency

Optimize resource allocation and project timeline planning.
Establish the team including project managers and development methodology.

4. Track Progress with Transparency and Consistency

Measure and monitor the progress on the overall strategy
Focus on delivering on strategy.

Make adjustment based on priority changes.

Recognize the common pitfalls and establish sound management controls, with a standardized set of guidelines for the projects. This ensures overall transparency and effective project execution.

OPM FUNDAMENTALS

Strategic Alignment

Innovation needs

Strategy and

Execution Alignment

>> *Diagram Innovation vs Execution* <<

Aligning portfolios and projects with corporate strategies and goals is the only way to ensure that your organization is focusing on the right projects. The organization needs to evaluate and align their strategies and project portfolios with business objectives to ensure they achieve the right outcomes.

How to manage Strategy and Execution Alignment:

Step 1: Plan Strategy Alignment
Step 2: Communicate Strategy
Step 3: Execute Strategy Alignment

Step 1: Plan Strategy Alignment

You must always ask two very important questions at the beginning:

1) What will your customers buy?
2) What are you producing?

A sustainable business model can only be realized through the pursuit of alignment.

Strategy communication and implementation will have a viable foundation with the full alignment. If the leadership team ignores and fails to ask these two questions, it will end up neglecting or not seeing at all the obvious and devastating misalignments. If misalignments are not addressed, we just cannot move forward without making necessary adjustments.

The business objective is to remain focused on the core competency while at the same time making reasonable attempts to satisfy the demands of the target business market.

The organization must analyze all high-priority strategic objectives, constraints, assumptions and relevant data to help program managers make informed decisions about what projects are needed and which deliverables are most beneficial to end users.

OPM is the strategic plan's execution framework, essential if the organization is developing innovative products, technologies, etc. It asks support for cross-functional efforts that provide a holistic view to the participating areas such as Engineering, Marketing, Finance or Manufacturing. This helps all stakeholders better understand the strategic goals and how their contributions will move the organization to the next level.

Strategically aligning the operations portfolio allows an organization to establish an execution approach which will:

- improve existing processes and

- optimize the selection and sequence of initiatives.

Leaders should define, screen, filter, and select programs and projects based on the organizational strategy and, for those selected, they should define:

- Roles and responsibilities
Define who will be involved, as well as each person's level of involvement and authority.

- Stakeholders
Who will be impacted by the initiatives and their level of influence in the organization.

- Resources
What resources could be assigned to programs and projects, and their current capacity and capabilities to support the selected initiatives.

- Funding
What funds will be available to implement the selected programs and projects.

- Risks
What internal and external risks would affect the strategic plan and therefore the portfolio of projects, and what risks will be accepted or mitigated.

- Benefits Realization
What benefits will be produced by each program and how those will be harvested.

To achieve that alignment, the following Groups must support the initiative:

- **Executive Group:** This group will provide the strategic and portfolio governance guidelines.

- **Project Group:** This group will handle portfolio management, focusing on delivering value to the business.

- **Operations Group:** This group will ensure the organization can sustainably achieve its strategic goals.

Step 2: Communicate Your Strategy

After creating a sound strategy based on customer desires and company core competency, leadership must align daily decisions and actions with the strategic direction. Employees and all functions are required to be fully aligned with their goals and actions.

Many projects fail due to the lack of a clear and effective communication management. The organization must develop an operations portfolio management plan that is closely aligned with organization's strategy, governance, risk management and performance management.

The strategy communication drives the full alignment necessary for the success of achieving organization's objectives.

Effective communication is a critical process between stakeholders, customers, management and everyone involved in OPM within your organization.

I have included a section on OPM communication management. It covers details about,

(1) Establish an OPM Communication Plan.

(2) Manage Portfolio Contents for Communication Management.

Step 3: Execute Strategy Alignment

This is very important step of the process that can produce desired business outcomes.

If you stop short of accomplishing this step you will not only fail to move forward strategically, you will also crush the expectations raised in the previous steps.

This is why most organizations end up damaging important cultural components such as trust and employee engagement.

At the end of the day, this step is just hard because the magnitude of change and innovation required to bridge the knowing/doing gap is so enormous.

To increase your chances of success, you will need to help your workforce support the following alignment behaviors:

- Make tough choices and difficult trade-offs that will deploy finite resources toward new behaviors, processes and practices (and away from older, less strategic areas).

- Innovate in ways that are responsive to the market you seek to serve. This customer-centricity is at the heart of alignment, and must become the focus of this change effort.

- Reduce operating costs while increasing sales. This will assure sustainability.

- Recognize and reward those who adopt new behaviors and decision-making approaches based on aligned priorities.

- Differentiate your company's offerings from that of the competition, thereby becoming more attractive to prospects while making competitors less so.

>> *Diagram Strategic Alignment* <<

Governance

Operations Portfolio management without governance is an empty concept.

Effective governance starts with leadership, commitment, and support from the top. However, leadership, while crucial, is not enough. You must define an appropriate organizational structure and outline the roles and responsibilities for all participants.

There are four main organizational components:

- executive leadership,

- the operations portfolio management team,
- program and project managers, and
- resource management.

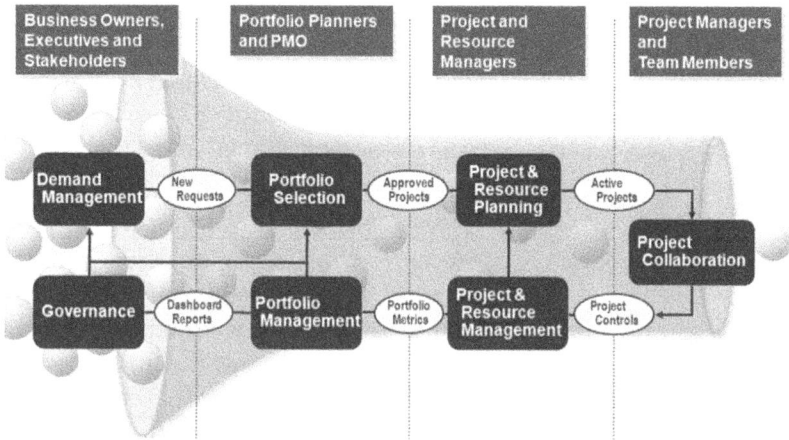

>> *Operations Portfolio Management R&R* <<

The table below defines some of the basic roles and responsibilities that will most likely need to be established. You'll need to tailor this based on the size of your organization and the complexity of your OPM.

Role	Responsibilities
Executive Team	Decision-making and oversight group, composed of senior executives. Responsibilities include championing the Portfolio Management process. The group sets portfolio funding levels, approves project recommendations, and provides policy guidance.

Operations Portfolio Management Team	The operations portfolio management and competency center, composed of the Portfolio Manager, Portfolio Administrator, and others with broad knowledge of organizational projects, such as impacted Program Managers. Responsible for the portfolio management process.
Portfolio Manager	Head of the Operations Portfolio Management Team. Oversees health, integration and delivery of projects within the portfolio. Responsibilities include communicating with project managers, making project recommendations, and reporting to the Executive Team.
Portfolio Administrator	Individual responsible for collecting project information, applying tools, and coordinating the day-to-day steps of the operations portfolio management process. Tracks portfolio details and provides summary views of project status.
Program Managers	Persons responsible for managing groups of projects with similar characteristics or directed at specific goals (e.g., capital projects, maintenance projects, customer-support projects, etc.). Responsibilities include verifying project cost, value, and risk estimates for projects within their respective programs.
Project Managers	Persons responsible for day-to-day management of individual projects. Responsibilities include providing project proposal data and communicating project status to Program Managers and the Portfolio Manager.
Resource Managers	Persons concerned with capacity management. Responsible for supplying skilled resources for conducting approved projects.

>> *Table Roles & Responsibilities* <<

Successful companies rely on tightly scripted meetings, objective analyses and decision frameworks to unite executives around a common vision. Consequently, they roll out failsafe, architecturally-

56

aligned projects which use the optimal amount of resources and deliver value.

Demand Management

Demand management is a planning methodology used to forecast, plan for and manage the demand for products and services. This can be at macro-levels as in economics and at micro-levels within individual organizations. Demand management is the process an organization puts in place to internally collect new ideas, projects, and needs during the creation of a portfolio.

There are many challenges in Demand Management,

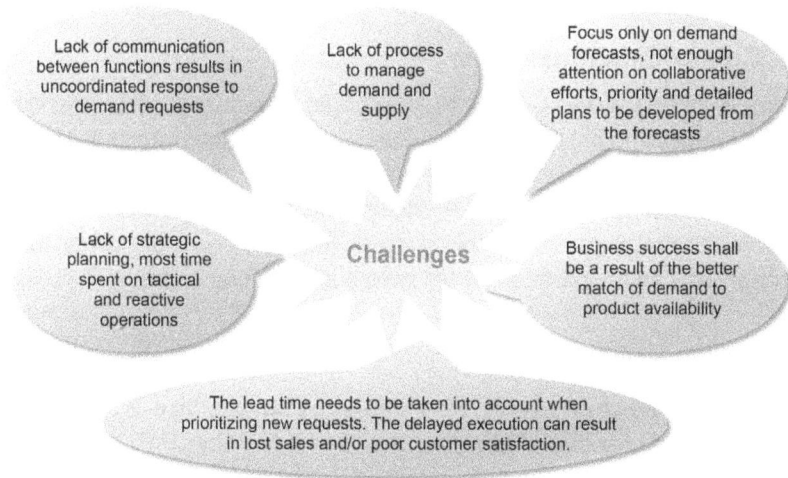

Lack of communication between functions results in uncoordinated response to demand requests

Lack of process to manage demand and supply

Focus only on demand forecasts, not enough attention on collaborative efforts, priority and detailed plans to be developed from the forecasts

Lack of strategic planning, most time spent on tactical and reactive operations

Challenges

Business success shall be a result of the better match of demand to product availability

The lead time needs to be taken into account when prioritizing new requests. The delayed execution can result in lost sales and/or poor customer satisfaction.

>> *Chart Demand Management Challenges* <<

OPM demands balancing limited resource availability with the ever increasing demand for those resources. It will also ensure that these limited resources are allocated to the initiatives that bring the most value to the organization as whole.

Initiatives across all lines of business need to be prioritized along with resource availability information in order to understand the organization's capacity for taking on initiatives.

Questions leadership must always ask,

- Are we investing in right things?
- How well are we executing?
- Are we optimizing our capacity?
- Are we realizing promised benefits?
- Can we absorb all the changes?

3 Essential Areas for Successful Demand Management

There are 3 key areas that need to be addressed for demand management to be successful.

1. Cross-Functional Team

First, a **cross-functional team** should be established to prioritize all initiatives against one another. This "prioritization committee" should have a member from all business groups and supporting organizations. When selecting members for the prioritization committee, choose people that are able think "big picture" or corporate-wide rather than ones who can only focus on their own business unit's needs.

2. Process to Prioritize

Second, a process should be established to prioritize all business initiatives against one another;

We can use a "prioritization matrix" to measure the impact each initiative has on the organization across predefined evaluation criteria. If the right criteria are chosen and every initiative is scored against those criteria by the cross-functional prioritization committee, the most important initiatives to the organization as a whole will become apparent.

An important tip is to ensure that not only the solutions being implemented are prioritized, but the initiatives to evaluate, select, or determine a solution are also prioritized. Many times organizations invest investing significant effort in selecting solutions for business that do not provide significant organizational value and should either be deferred or stopped altogether.

I've given you a sample selection criteria table options below to help you with this critical step. There is also a project bubble diagram which gives a visual representation of where each project lies within the risk/value quadrants.

These will help you quickly and easily see those projects that should be pursued and those with a risk/value ratio that would be unacceptable to your organization.

Prioritization Criteria	SCORE		
	1 point	3 points	5 points
Strategy Delivery	Low 1 objective	Medium 2-3 objectives	High 4 or more objectives
Product Synergies	Low new product with new sales, support and manufacturing	Medium new product with existing sales	High new product with existing sales, support and manufacturing
Profitability	Minor NPV < $1M	Medium $1M < NPV < $5M	Major NPV > $5M
Technical Viability	Very Difficult Major technical obstacles to be resolved	Somewhat Difficult Need to resolve 1 - 3 technical difficulties	Easy No known technical issues
Product Marketability	Low Very few inquires	Medium Several requests of product info	High High interest of the new product
Competition & IP Protection	High Many competitors No IP Protection	Medium 3 - 5 competitors IP Protected	Low 0 - 2 competitors Strong IP Protected
Resources Required	High > 2,000 man-hours, need external resources for more than $100K	Medium 500 - 2,000 man-hours, need external resources between $50K - $100K	Low Less than 500 man-hours and no external resources
Risks	High Regulatory, financial, technical or operational risks	Medium Some regulatory, financial, technical or operational risks	Low Minimum regulatory, financial, technical or operational risks

>> Chart Table Selection Criteria <<

3. Resource Availability

Third, focus on **resource availability** once the solution evaluation/selection or solution implementation initiative has been prioritized. Once an initiative scores high enough to warrant moving forward, resource availability needs to be analyzed. It is important that employees with subject matter expertise and critical skills track their time and forecast future anticipated time expenditures.

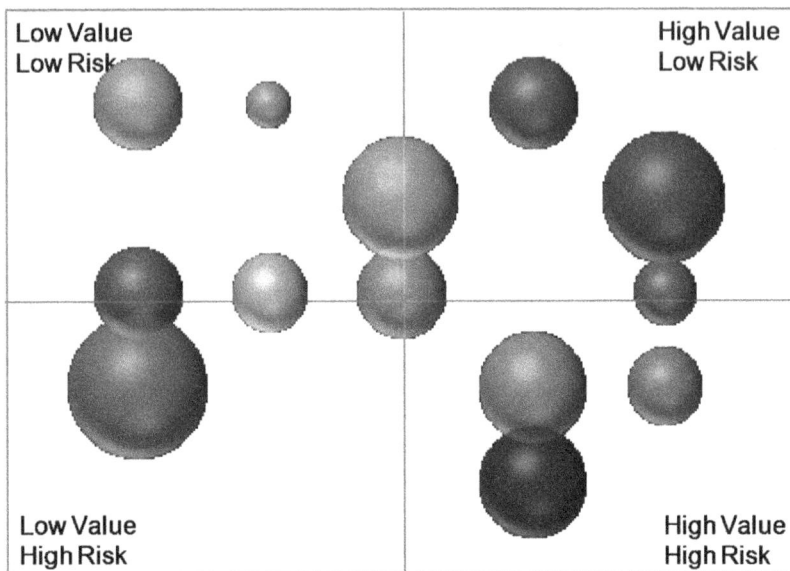

Low Value Low Risk	High Value Low Risk
Low Value High Risk	High Value High Risk

>> *Chart Portfolio Bubble Chart* <<

Additionally, there should be categories for administrative, operational, or **"keep the lights on" (KTLO) activities.**

It is critical that you clearly define what is considered KTLO efforts as anything that is not KTLO should be submitted to the prioritization committee for prioritization. This is important as it eliminates the subjective definition of what a project is and enables more granular insight and control over where resources are spending their time.

Once resource availability is understood, the prioritization committee can assign resources and a start date to the initiative or develop resource remediation options for situations where resource constraints exist.

Remediation Options could include changing the start date of the new initiative, putting another initiative on hold to start the new one, or bringing in additional resources in order to fulfill resource demands. Once the options are collaboratively identified by the prioritization committee, the options should be escalated to an executive steering committee (made up of business executives) to decide on a remediation approach.

Effective Operations Portfolio Management practices places accountability for the prioritization of initiatives and the remediation of resource constraints (including the allocation of additional funding if necessary) on the business.

If accomplished, the management of business demand and resource supply to meet the goals and objectives of the organization can be attained. When the business can manage this balance between supply and demand, a nimbler, efficient, and effective organization to meet the ever changing business needs is created to drive maximum business value.

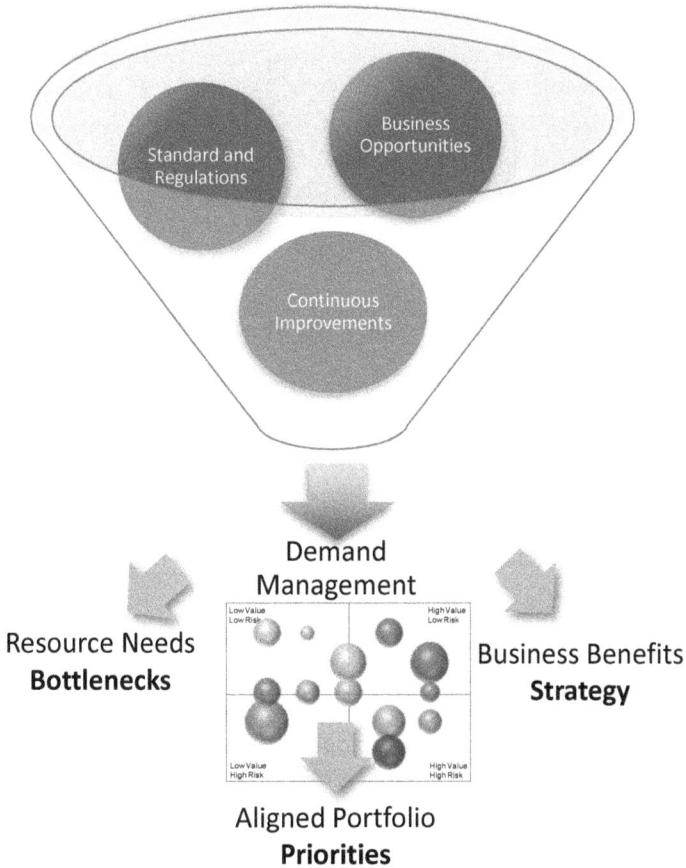

>> *Diagram Demand Management Flow 1* <<

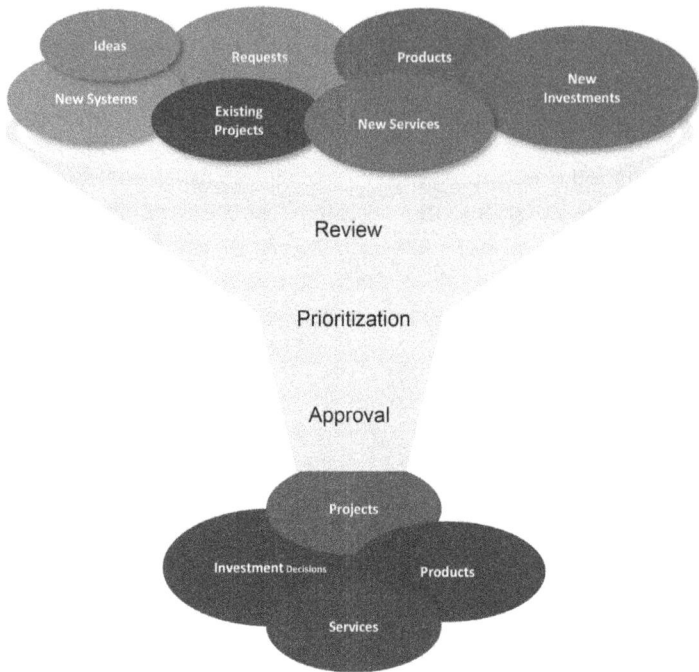

Review

Prioritization

Approval

>> *Diagram Demand Management Flow 2* <<

Resource Management

When Resource Management is used in reference to Portfolio/Program/ Project management, resource management often applies to resource leveling and smoothing.

Resource leveling is designed to avoid shortages or excess inventory by keeping the stock of resources at a level that avoids both problems.

It's also used in reference to the time it takes to complete a project. With leveling, the start and finish dates are adjusted so that they mesh with resource availability. Leveling might extend the project timeline.

Resource smoothing is a scheduling technique that attempts to meet a specified deadline while avoiding peaks and valleys on the resources.

The goal is a constant use of resources over time.

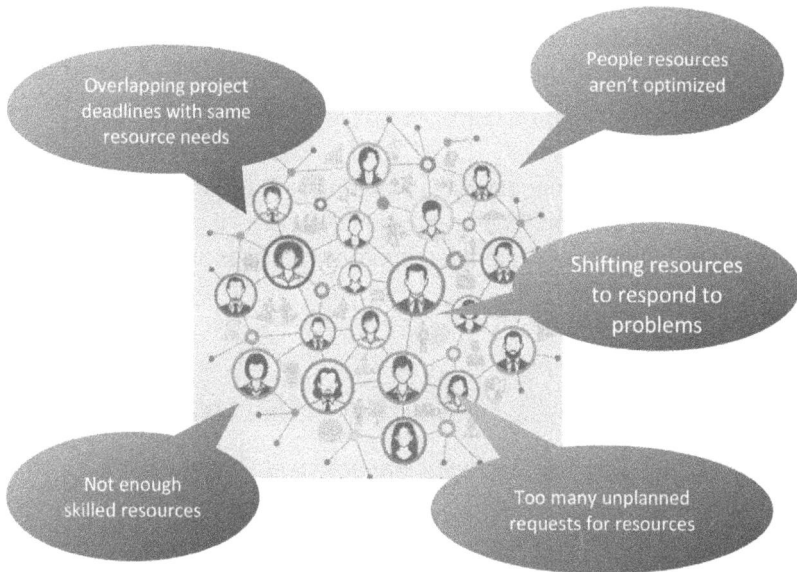

>> *Diagram Resource Management Challenges* <<

Resource Management is about making sure that a company is using its talents and materials wisely and effectively.

Guidelines for Effective Resource Management:

- Create a centralized resource tracking list across all projects and services. It will provide good visibility on resource utilization and availability.

- Define a list of skillset associated to resources. The project management team can establish a team based on resource availability to deliver on these projects. Prioritize resources and group them in different buckets so that the management can easily assign them to prioritized projects.

- Establish a master schedule of all resources to manage various resource workloads and identify resource conflicts.

- Implement a contingent workforce strategy to address current and upcoming resource shortages. It allows for backup plan when unexpected changes happen.

- Provide visibility of resource capacity during Portfolio Prioritization. It also provides visibility to business functions on their staffing status and needs. The Portfolio Prioritization will facilitate better pipeline and staffing for current and future projects.

- Leverage technologies to streamline Resource Management with integration to Prioritization Process. It provides a more structured and systematic approach to Resource Management and Planning.

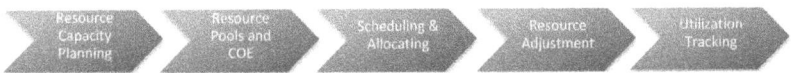

>> Diagram Resource Management Process <<

Strategic Resource Allocation

The following guidelines will help leadership make resource allocation decisions which are well informed and advance the organization.

- Avoid peanut butter spreading or over staffing
Initiatives with potential are not given sufficient resources to support proper execution within an expected timeframe. An activity supported by too few resources is set up to fail.

If there are enough resources to fund all of the good ideas submitted, is it wise to do so? What happens if all available capital is committed at the beginning of the cycle and a better project emerges mid-cycle? Sometimes it is necessary to say no to good ideas to preserve flexibility for new opportunities.

- Align and adopt a limited number of prioritization criteria
Develop prioritization criteria using a process that includes key stakeholders. The alignment on Prioritization Criteria is essential. If the process by which criteria are developed is not perceived as credible or inclusive, it is very likely that results will be perceived as flawed or biased.

Using too many criteria makes it more difficult to surface a small list of

64

winning proposals. In addition, overlapping criteria may result in one element being over weighted in the prioritization process.

- Challenge the resource needs and assess alternatives
It is worth to ask:

- Are these resources really necessary?

- Can the result be accomplished through other less expensive efforts?

- What alternatives were considered?

It is really up to the senior leadership to ensure that these questions have been raised and thought through.

- Find the critical path
Many large initiatives are really a series of smaller projects.

An innovation product involves a number of individual components. An information technology strategy involves a series of configurations. For any series of investments, it is important to understand the critical path of decision making to determine the importance of individual components and the timing for investment in them.

Communication Management

What is Operations Portfolio Communication Management?

>> Portfolio Communication Management Diagram <<

65

There are many aspects of a portfolio. Effective communication is a critical process between stakeholders, customers, management and everyone involved in Operations Portfolio Management. Many projects failed due to the lack of a clear and effective communication management. The organization must develop an operations portfolio management plan that is closely aligned with organization's strategy, governance, risk management and performance management.

An effective communication management needs to consider the following:

- Contents of information to be communicated
- Level of details and method to be communicated considering confidential level and IP protection
- Sequence of general portfolio and specific project communication
- Schedule and timing of the communication
- Responsible party for regular portfolio and project communication
- Communication requirements including contents, distribution, frequency and method
- Communication method for communication process changes
- Escalation process in case issues to be addressed and resolved
- Standard communication templates to be used in communication management
- Understand constraints and dependencies affecting communication

There are **2 Stages of Communication Management**.

(1) Establish an OPM Communication Plan.

(2) Manage Portfolio Contents for Communication Management.

(1) Establish an OPM Communication Plan

Communication at this stage focuses on engagement of all stakeholders. It is very important to get them fully involved to define the communication flow and get their input on communication contents. In addition, this wide communication strategy will help you identify potential risks and dependencies along with risk mitigation plan.

The organization needs to identify all portfolio stakeholders and their communication requirements. Stakeholders can be internal to the organization as well as external stakeholders.

As part of the planning process, roles and responsibilities are defined and clarified for managing communication. For example, groups involved in Communication Management Planning could include executive sponsors, executive steering committee, key business stakeholders, change control board, program managers, project managers, subject matter experts, and external consultants. Depending on organization's portfolio needs, it will include some or all of these groups.

As part of developing a Portfolio Communication Plan, all stakeholders must be identified, especially primary stakeholders and executives with interests in these projects.

Table of Contents

>> *Sample Communication Plan 1* <<

Also, be sure to identify and confirm executive sponsors who will be accountable for the success of organization's portfolio and each individual project. It is quite common for additional stakeholders to be needed, or have changes in original stakeholders.

The Communication Management Plan will be updated based on these changes.

When all stakeholders are identified, the Plan will determine the level of information to be communicated and the communication methods.

(2) Manage Portfolio Contents for Communication Management

After collecting communication requirements from all stakeholders, the process will cover gathering, sorting and distributing relevant Portfolio Contents to stakeholders, based on predefined distribution list, frequency and level of details. The type of communication could include project kick-off, regular executive update, project status report, design review and deep-dive for projects with concerns and risks.

Communication distribution could follow predefined communication matrix that teams can follow.

For example,

- If this is a general communication, follow general communication distribution list and predefined communication template.
- If this is not for general communication, determine the confidential level and specific distribution list. Also, the executive needs to review and approve contents before they can be distributed.
- If it is unclear whether the contents are confidential or not, a decision from the executive is required, and then distribute contents accordingly.

Many organizations use a variety portal platforms such as Sharepoint and Jive for corporate wide collaboration and communication.

It is highly recommended to utilize organization's portal platform to provide the general communication and status of a project or a portfolio.

Communication	Objective of Communications	Media	Frequency	Participants	Owner	Deliverable
Project Workgroup Meetings	Develop high level project plans and protocols	- Face to Face - Conference Call - Webex	Weekly	- Project Team	- Project Manager - Project Lead	- Agenda - Project Schedule - Project Updates
Project Committee Meetings	Review status of the project	- Face to Face - Webex	Monthly	- Project Committee	- Project Manager - Project Lead	- Agenda - Project Schedule - Project Updates
Weekly Technical Review Meetings	Discuss and develop technical design solutions for the project	- Face to Face - Webex	Weekly or As Needed	- PMO Team	- PMO Head	- Agenda - Project Schedule - Project Decisions
Weekly PMO Status Report	Project status updates and work plans	- Face to Face - Conference Call - Webex	Weekly	- PMO Head	- PMs	- Agenda - Project Updates
Stakeholder Meeting	Program management and monitoring	- Face to Face - Conference Call - Webex	Monthly	- Stakeholders	- PMO Head	- Agenda - Project Updates
Partner Coordination Meetings	Overall project status report, coordination of responsibilities and discussion	- Face to Face - Webex	Bi-weekly	- PMO - Partner Management - PM	- PMO	- Agenda - Project Updates

>> Sample Communication Plan 2 <<

Details about Portfolio Communication Management

Portfolio Communication provides extract and summary information, unlike project managers who provide detailed project related status, issues and risks. The main focus of portfolio communication is always delivery appropriate messages on strategy.

The Portfolio Communication strategy must ensure all stakeholders understand the portfolio and its associated strategy and objectives. The communication on the progress of a portfolio execution is constantly managed and level of contents are properly controlled. Also, metrics and KPIs (Key Performance Indicators) are established and reported on a regular base.

There are many functions, stakeholders, executives, project managers involved in a Portfolio. It is important to establish a comprehensive communication matrix so that the right level of contents can be communicated to everyone involved. The Communication Plan needs to consider many kinds of activities such as emails, messages, meetings, metrics reporting, status update, escalation and Go-No Go decisions.

As organizations become more remote and virtualized, the Operations Portfolio management team has to evaluate and decide the value of its contents and communication path. Communication can be a Discussion, an Action Assignment, or a Request/Response Interaction. It is crucial to maintain the consistent communication from Operations Portfolio management; it helps build the trust among all stakeholders as well as improve the communication efficiency.

It is always important to communicate the portfolio strategy to entire organization. Senior executives create the message emphasizing the importance of the strategy, and then pass on to all stakeholders, all management layers and project team members who are involved in the portfolio delivering the strategy.

With communication management plan, metrics will be established and the right level of messages are passed to all level of groups and functions.

The Operations Portfolio Management needs to be very clear on the communication objectives, shareholder expectations, culture diversity, regulation constraints, and distribution mechanism.

There are many methods and tools available for communication management. A dashboard approach is commonly used method.

The dashboard presents Portfolio contents in a visual graphic manner. It presents the information using Bar Chart, Pie Chart, Gantt Chart, Trend Lines, Color coded status like Red, Yellow and Green. Also, the graph can compare target numbers versus actual numbers, and show delta for discrepancy or missed milestone dates. Typically, it is much easier and quicker for people to understand the contents with charts, colors and graphics.

It will be much more efficient if these dashboard data are constantly updated in real time. If possible, the dashboard should also allow management to drill down into next level details.

For example, when a Program has some issues, management can drill further down to projects within the Program to understand which project might be the main cause impacting the overall progress of a program for the portfolio. This also helps the information to be shared consistently by presenting a single source of truth for everyone involved.

In the event of portfolio changes, Operations Portfolio Management team needs to develop a roadmap meeting new requirements and making adjustment on existing process and criteria. Also, project managers are properly trained on communication technologies, communication process and contents creations. The Operations Portfolio Management will evaluate and adjust the Communication Plan to improve the communication effectiveness.

Develop a Portfolio Stakeholder Matrix

allows management to understand how key resources are positioned and deployed. It described different roles, constraints, level of commitment and contact information.

For example, a Portfolio Stakeholder Matrix list out Stakeholder name, function, specific goals, motivation, constraints, level of authority, and recommended engagement approach. Building a Stakeholder Matrix is essential to provide successful communication to stakeholders. Once a Stakeholder Matrix is established, Operations Portfolio Management can ensure contents are passed effectively on to all stakeholders.

Name	Role	Stakeholder's area of interest/concern/sensitivity and why	Level of support					Level of interest in the program			Level of influence on the program			Stakeholder's benefits from the program	Stakeholder's disbenefits from program	Who owns communication with the individual stakeholder	Comments
			Stronly supportive	Moderately supportive	Neutral	Moderately against	Stronly against	High	Medium	Low	Strong	Medium	Low				

Name	Role	Stakeholder's area of interest / concern / sensitivity and why	Level of support				
			Stronly supportive	Moderately supportive	Neutral	Moderately against	Stronly against

		Level of interest in the program			Level of influence on the program			Stakeholder's benefits from the program	Stakeholder's disbenefits from the program	Who owns communication with the individual stakeholder
		High	Medium	Low	Strong	Medium	Low			

>> Sample Stakeholder Register <<

71

Risk Management

Risk Management Defined

Any possible factor that might have a negative impact on Portfolio's objectives is considered a Portfolio Risk. The impact can be small or big, but often is unpredictable. The organization must eliminate these uncertainties as much as possible so that these risks won't derail the overall Portfolio objectives.

There is a strong need to have a process and structured approach to evaluate Portfolio Risk through Risk Management. Risk Management's goal is to mitigate events, activities, and conditions that will have a negative impact on Portfolio.

In a Portfolio, there are frequently some dependencies between programs and projects. This can mean that any significant impact on one project will have a negative impact on another project or program. In some cases, one Portfolio Risk can potentially increase the risk level of another risk. Therefore, Portfolio Risk Management become very important in identifying and dealing with these potential issues and their dependencies.

When a project is in execution stage, there are a few risk factors that need to be identified and mitigated. A Portfolio Risk Management Strategy needs to be developed for this purpose. Portfolio Risk Management will have a better understanding of overall risk for a portfolio and enable management to adjust individual project risks accordingly. This reduces the potential for one failed project to bring down an entire portfolio, for example.

Other than identifying potential issues and concerns, Portfolio Risk Management process can identify opportunities of improvements on product design, product delivery, service quality, and customer satisfaction. In some cases, new Portfolio components might be established through the discovery of Portfolio Risk Management.

Risk

- Risk is an uncertain event or event that might happen in future

- Once risk is identified, its impact should be analyzed and the response plan should be prepared

- Examples:
  Lack of Business knowledge which may impact the quality of workable products

Potential negative impact

Issue

- Issue is an event that has already occurred

- Once the impact of issue is analyzed, the same should be resolved or escalated

- Examples:
  Product scope changes require incremental spending not in original approved budget

Already impacting the cost, time and delivery

>> *Table Risk vs. Issue* <<

Reference ID	Date Reported	Risk Description	Likelihood	Impact	Risk Assessment	Owner	MitigationAction	Contigent Action	Progress on Actions	Status
1	2/5/18	The main supplier can not deliver on time because of other commitments	Low	High	High	John Doe	Include financial penalities in contract. Build contingency into the schedule. Monitor contractor performance.	Revised product rollout schedule.		Active

>> *Table Sample Risk Log* <<

73

Operations Portfolio Risk Management versus Project & Program Risk Management

Portfolio risk management recognizes and chooses the acceptable level of risk based on the anticipation of higher reward.

Project or program risk management focuses on identifying, evaluating and mitigating risks that can impact a project or a program. Risk management is avoiding failure for project or program.

For Portfolio Risk Management, an organization may invest in new technology that is unproven and untested, in anticipation of new market sales. The risk is that the technology may not work for the mass market as it is originally designed. However, the benefit is significant with a big pay off if the technology does work.

While project risks are specific to a program and project, Portfolio focuses on a portfolio entirely, taking into the considerations of financial value, alignment of objectives and strategy and the balance of different projects and programs within the portfolio.

Portfolio risk management is more difficult than project risk management. One formula that works for one project may not work for another. There is no one formula that will work for an entire portfolio. Portfolio risk management will have multiple ways to mitigate risks that will impact the strategic objectives of a portfolio, and increase the value, improve the overall fitness and have positive impact.

Overview of Portfolio Risk Management Processes

Portfolio Risk Management plays specific roles that can impact the overall portfolio. It is one of many Operations Portfolio Management Process. It involves **Risk Management Planning, Risk Assessment and Risk Mitigation.**

Risk Management Planning

During Portfolio Risk Management Planning, the tolerance of portfolio risks needs to be identified. This would help create next step of management of portfolio risks. An organization's portfolio may have many potential threats and risks. These risk conditions may either have a positive or negative impact at either organizational or component level.

74

For example, too many concurrent projects with dependency on limited core resources, have negative risks on the overall Portfolio. Another example, leveraging productivity and project management tools, getting highly skilled external resources, will have a positive impact.

To get an overall risk level controlled, the Portfolio Risk Management needs to come up a plan to handle the desirable risk level towards the positive side. For any risks, root causes must be understood and analyzed at both Portfolio and components level. The overall impact should be analyzed at Organization and Portfolio level.

In order to develop a Portfolio Risk Management Plan, first establish the structure of risk management activities and how these activities will be performed. Once the structure is created, complete with timeline, process, and reference to policies, guidelines and risk tolerances, thresholds and mitigation strategy.

The established Risk Management Plan will also serve as a framework and guideline when new portfolio components are added. The Portfolio Risk Management will review and determine whether these new components would increase the overall Portfolio Risk level. If the risk level is too high and thus not acceptable, management must either stop, change, suspend or accept the new project while developing additional activities within Risk Management Plan to mitigate the negative impact.

In the end, Portfolio Risk Management needs to balance achieving organization's objectives, and controlling organization's risks. Not only we need to do the projects right, but also we need to do the right projects.

Risk Assessment

Anyone in an organization can raise concerns on potential threats in organization's portfolio. It could be executive management, project management or stakeholders. These risks will vary based on their organizational level and their interpretation. The portfolio risk management will take a consistent approach to analyze these risks from various sources.

For example, executive management will pay more attention to the investment and return, time to market and strategic objectives. These cover brand name recognition, product launch and ongoing services. Executives focus more on establishing the company's core value, protecting shareholder's value and creating competitive edge. At the same time, the executive team has to understand liabilities and threats within Portfolio Risk Management Plan.

At a different level, operation management team is focusing more on issues related to services, product development, and resource alignment. The risk management for operations is on supporting smooth operations with minimum organizational changes.

For Project Portfolio Managers, concerns are around issues that could impact the alignment between organizational strategy and portfolio. Also, they will look at dashboard reporting, data quality and risks arising from individual component.

At Program and Project level, managers are more focused on scope, schedule, cost and execution quality at Portfolio's component level. These risks might be related to integration, dependency and transparency with other components.

Identify and track potential threats into Risk Log either in spreadsheet or an online system. Review these risks and understand the severity, impacts and probability.

Risk Mitigation

Once risks are tracked, mitigation options, actions and ownership need to be decided.

Throughout the portfolio risk management process, potential threats are monitored and controlled. Also, the status of existing risks will change. The management needs to make necessary adjustment accordingly.

It is important to identify where these risks come from. They may come from internal or external sources. Most of these risks are discovered during the Planning process.

Examples of **Internal Sources**:

- Priority changes
- Corporate Reorganizations

- Funding reallocation
- R&D advancement/delay
- New Programs/Projects
- Global locations

Corruption and bankruptcy are also considered as sources of internal risks.

Examples of **External Sources**:

- Product Market Competitions
- Financial and economic situations
- Legal and government regulatory requirements
- Political events
- Technology breakthrough
- Natural disasters

For potential threats, large efforts usually will be spent on data gathering, benchmark analysis, and competitive study. The findings can be either a threat or an opportunity.

In addition, the management has to determine whether these potential threats are **structural** or **execution** risks.

Structural Risks

Structural risks are obstacles impacting organization's ability to effectively manage its portfolio. There are organizational hierarchical and matrix structure for carrying out their operations and tasks.

Without a proper organizational alignment, the operations portfolio management will become ineffective and inefficient. A portfolio plan that is overly aggressive, or subject to frequent strategy changes will also have a big threats to a portfolio itself. Establishing an effective portfolio governance utilizing best practices will become a positive opportunity.

Execution Risks

Execution Risks are issues related to portfolio execution or its components such as Programs or Projects. In Portfolio Risk Management, it is important to evaluate the ability to manage changes, the ability to execute the plan, and the ability to align with other components to deliver on strategies. The common challenges are interaction between different programs and projects. It is very important to utilize templates and system tools to manage interdependency of multiple components.

Risk Tolerance

The organization needs to identify its risk aversion threshold. Based on the data analysis, a Portfolio can be identified as Risk Tolerant or Risk Intolerant.

An organization could take more risks to increase impact and probability of positive results. For example, it will move more quickly to roll out new product with heavy investment on manufacturing capacity, while the other functions such as services and existing products will be impacted negatively.

For a Risk Tolerant organization, with a balanced Portfolio Risk Management Plan, an organization will take calculated risks, without losing sight of the overall benefits that all components could generate.

For a Risk Intolerant organization, the management would prefer a minimum risk Portfolio. In reality, it is often impractical, as a Portfolio as well as Programs and Projects will encounter risks one way or the other.

Portfolio Manager and Risk Management

Operations Portfolio management is an important way to implement strategic initiatives.

Portfolio Managers:

- manage one or more portfolios (groups of projects or programs)
- align programs, projects and operations to strategic objectives; and

78

- measure, rank and prioritize programs and projects.

Apart from above responsibilities, a Portfolio Manager also needs to mitigate risks and provide contingencies and alternatives when something goes wrong. The Portfolio Manager must be able to manage contingencies to mitigate threats with low probability and high impact.

The purpose of Portfolio Risk Management is to reduce the impact of potential threats, and increase the chance of positive impacts. It needs to balance risks and rewards, it needs to balance the shifting priorities and effective execution. It also supports decisions about trade-offs among programs and projects to achieve a strategically healthy portfolio.

Performance Management

Although Operations Portfolio Management does not guarantee success, an effective Performance Management process certainly increases the potential for achieving the organization's goals and objectives.

- Evaluate and prioritize the projects that best support strategic objectives,

- Track and monitor performance during execution to ensure all portfolio components are on track to deliver strategic goals

- Adjust priority and the portfolio based on strategy changes and ongoing performance

Candidate projects are tracked and mapped to organization's strategic objectives. These projects are prioritized against all other projects already in the queue or ongoing. This allows all stakeholders to determine the relative priorities of these projects with respect to objectives they support. In many cases, the projects selected for the portfolio contain the balance crossing competing organizational objectives. The projects in the portfolio provide best total relative benefits to available budget, resource constraints and project dependencies.

Making portfolio decisions is an iterative process. The process involves reviewing both quantitative and qualitative factors. Typically, each objective should have a solid numeric weight with respect to other objectives. Also, each project in the portfolio should have a solid relative benefit matching to a specific organization's goals.

The organization needs to monitor and manage the overall portfolio and its performance. Performance metrics need to be established and warning criteria defined. Also, a performance baseline should be established along with a reporting process. To evaluate the performance at the portfolio level, it is important to measure individual projects and consolidate the measurements into a systematic manner, so that these measurements reflect the fitness of the portfolio.

For all projects, the metrics need to monitor the performance related to cost, schedule, and scope. In addition, the metrics need to evaluate whether these projects on the portfolio remain on track to deliver the strategic goals and objectives.

Quite often strategic objectives are conflicting with each other. For example, investing in manufacturing capacity for immediate production volumes versus more R&D Investment.

In order to address these competing objectives, we need to establish conflict decision strategy to allow us make trade-offs. If short term sales are more important, we may go ahead with the expansion of manufacturing capacity. If long term growth has a higher priority, we may need to invest more on R&D.

A good analogy is buying airline tickets. If time is more important, we will choose non-stop direct flight with higher cost. If price is more important, we may choose low cost flight with multiple stops.

Given the stated organization's goals and objectives, management needs to determine what matters most to the organization now and in the future, and what are its priorities now and over the next two to five years.

AHP - Analytic Hierarchy Process

Many organizations use Analytic Hierarchy Process (**AHP**) to define relative strategic benefits for projects in a portfolio.

Analytic Hierarchy Process (AHP) is one of Multi Criteria decision making methods originally developed by Prof. Thomas L. Saaty.

Briefly, it is a method to derive ratio scales from paired comparisons. The input can be obtained from actual measurement such as price, weight etc., or from subjective opinion such as satisfaction feelings and preference. AHP allow some small inconsistency in judgment because human is not always consistent. The ratio scales are derived from the principal Eigen vectors and the consistency index is derived from the principal Eigen value.

Mathematically the method is based on the solution of an Eigen value problem. The results of the pair-wise comparisons are arranged in a matrix. The first (dominant) normalized right Eigen vector of the matrix gives the ratio scale (weighting), the Eigen value determines the consistency ratio.

AHP has a lot more details and will be covered separately.

NPV - Net Present Value

Weighting and scoring are often used when there are multiple criteria, for example, least cost and highest **NPV**.

NPV stands for **Net Present Value** and is the difference between the present value of cash inflows and the present value of cash outflows. NPV is used in capital budgeting to analyze the profitability of a project investment.

Example 1: Even Cash Inflows: Calculate the **net present value** of a project which requires an initial investment of $243,000 and it is expected to generate a cash inflow of $50,000 each month for 12 months. Assume that the salvage value of the project is zero. The target rate of return is 12% per annum.

Solution

We have,
Initial Investment = $243,000
Net Cash Inflow per Period = $50,000
Number of Periods = 12
Discount Rate per Period = 12% ÷ 12 = 1%

Net Present Value
= $50,000 × (1 − (1 + 1%)^-12) ÷ 1% − $243,000

= \$50,000 × (1 − 1.01^-12) ÷ 0.01 − \$243,000
≈ \$50,000 × (1 − 0.887449) ÷ 0.01 − \$243,000
≈ \$50,000 × 0.112551 ÷ 0.01 − \$243,000
≈ \$50,000 × 11.2551 − \$243,000
≈ \$562,754 − \$243,000
≈ \$319,754

Example 2: Uneven Cash Inflows: An initial investment of \$8,320 thousand on plant and machinery is expected to generate cash inflows of \$3,411 thousand, \$4,070 thousand, \$5,824 thousand and \$2,065 thousand at the end of first, second, third and fourth year respectively. At the end of the fourth year, the machinery will be sold for \$900 thousand. Calculate the net present value of the investment assuming the discount rate is 18%. Round your answer to nearest thousand dollars.

Solution

PV Factors:
Year 1 = 1 ÷ (1 + 18%)^1 ≈ 0.8475
Year 2 = 1 ÷ (1 + 18%)^2 ≈ 0.7182
Year 3 = 1 ÷ (1 + 18%)^3 ≈ 0.6086
Year 4 = 1 ÷ (1 + 18%)^4 ≈ 0.5158

The rest of the calculation is summarized below:

Year	1	2	3	4
Net Cash Inflow	\$3,411	\$4,070	\$5,824	\$2,065
Salvage Value				900
Total Cash Inflow	\$3,411	\$4,070	\$5,824	\$2,965
× Present Value Factor	0.8475	0.7182	0.6086	0.5158
Present Value of Cash Flows	\$2,890.68	\$2,923.01	\$3,544.67	\$1,529.31
Total PV of Cash Inflows	\$10,888			
− Initial Investment	− 8,320			
Net Present Value	\$2,568 thousand			

Net present value (NPV) of a project is the potential change in an investor›s wealth caused by that project while time value of money is being accounted for. It equals the present value of net cash inflows generated by a project less the initial investment on the project. It is one of the most reliable measures used in capital budgeting because it accounts for time value of money by using discounted cash flows in the calculation.

EVM - Earned Value Management

Many organizations use **EVM** to monitor program and project progress. **EVM** stands for

Earned Value Management, a project management technique for measuring project performance and progress in an objective manner.

Earned Value Management (EVM) helps project managers to measure project performance. It is a systematic project management process used to find variances in projects based on the comparison of worked performed and work planned. EVM is used on the cost and schedule control and can be very useful in project forecasting.

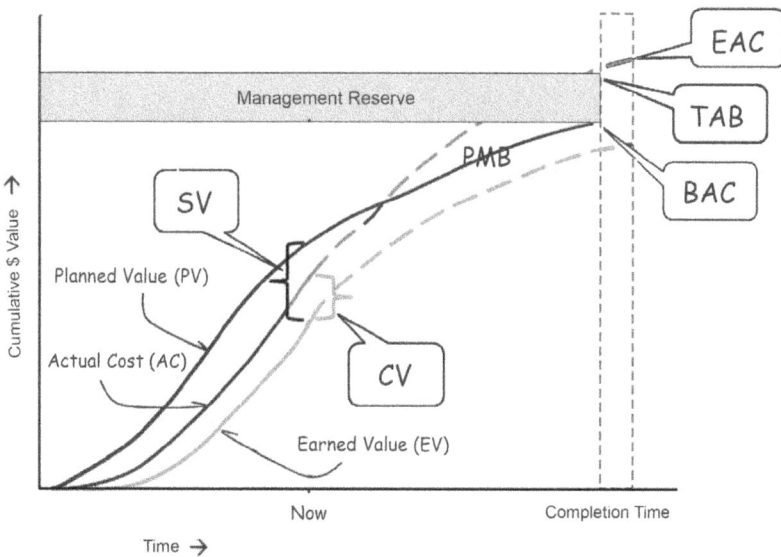

>> Chart Earned Value Management <<

SV – Schedule Variance. It is the difference between how much of schedule for an activity is actually utilized versus how much of schedule should have been utilized.

PV – Planned Value. This is the authorized budget allocated for the given. This is allocated over the entire duration of phase or project.

AC – Actual Cost. This is the actual amount of budget spent in carrying out the work on any given activity at any given point in time.

CV – Cost Variance. It is the difference between how much of budget for an activity is actually utilized versus how much of budget should have been utilized.

EV – Earned Value. This is the actual value of work performed on any given activity at any given point in time. This is expressed in terms of approved budget for that activity.

BAC – Budget at Completion. This is the total planned value for ALL activities over the entire project. In other words, this is the planned amount you will end up spending on project work when the project ends. We say 'planned' because BAC is calculated during planning period, which is much ahead of project completion time.

EAC – Estimate at Completion. This is calculated at a given point in time based on how much of work on an activity is complete. This is a measure of expected cost of activity when it finally completes. EAC can be different from BAC.

TAB – Total Allocated Budget. Also known as Total project funds. This is the sum of all activity-level budget on the project – performance management baseline (PMB) + management reserve.

PMB – Total Planned Value is sometime referred to as Performance Measurement Baseline. PMB is the time-phased budget plan for accomplishing work, against which contract performance is measured. Note that this does NOT contain management reserve.

The production of EV data requires that a performance measurement baseline, drawn directly from the project plan, comprising of the following:

- The **Performance Measurement Baseline (PM**B): The PMB consists of a time-phased aggregation of the (human and material) resources required to execute the work scope of the project, usually in a Work Breakdown Structure (WBS) **and within which we would perform EV analysis. The PMB is often shown as a cumulative X/Y curve (as in the above diagram)**. This is the 'baseline' against which cost and schedule performance is compared using EVM metrics. The full PMB should also include and define how Earned Value will be measured and taken through the life of the project.

- **Objective Measures of Progress**: Progress must be assessed periodically – there are many ways of doing this and the important rule (backed up by a mass of evidence) is that the more subjective the methods are, the less reliable the EV data is likely to be and the greater room there is for unwanted 'surprises' downstream.

- **Actual Costs – Labor and Materials: Actual cost data must then be gathered against by the elements in the PMB – this** requires that business systems and processes enable useful and timely capture of actual cost data, via the structures that are employed in the EVM system – not something that falls naturally from all business systems.

The objective is to embed EV data into the practice of daily management of the project, leading to an improvement in decision-making based upon an informed analysis of real status against cost and schedule goals, at the working levels of the project.

While earned value management provides a useful and powerful method for capturing project cost and schedule performance, it does not account for meeting specifications or the customer's expectations. A project can be performing well in terms of cost and schedule, but if the project is not meeting specifications or customer expectations, then project success is negatively affected.

Earned Value Components

> Planned Value (a.k.a. BCWS)

- How much work (person-hours) you planned to have accomplished at a given point in time (this is from the WBS in your plan)

> Actual Cost (a.k.a. ACWP)

- How much work (person-hours) you have actually spent at a given point in time

> Earned Value (a.k.a. BCWP)

- The value (person-hours) in terms of your base budget of what you have accomplished at a given point in time (or, % complete X Planned Value)

Earned Value: Example

Day X

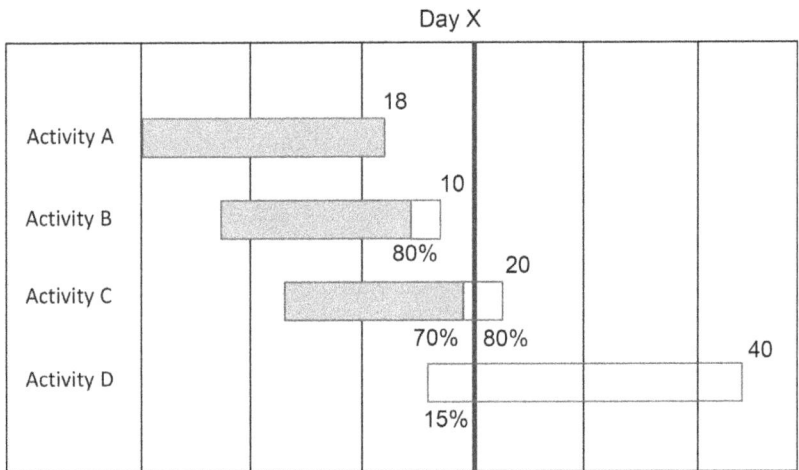

>> Chart Earned Value Sample <<

On Day X:

> PLANNED VALUE (Budgeted cost of the work scheduled, BCWS) =
18 + 10 + 16 + 6 = 50

86

> EARNED VALUE (Budgeted cost of the work performed, BCWP) =
> 18 + 8 + 14 + 0 = 40

> ACTUAL COST (of the work performed, ACWP) =
> 45 (from your project tracking - not evident in above chart)

QPI - Quality Performance Index

Quality Performance Index (QPI) could be used as a measure of how well the result of a project appears to be conforming to original requirements, or specifications. The Quality Performance Index (QPI) is a measure of consistency in the application of the Project Standards and Procedures as well as the compliance of the delivered product with the project specifications.

In many cases, a rating review by a subject matter expert can be used for quality check. For example, a rating of 9 of 10 would mean that conformance to requirements is 90%.

Another way is validating deliverables directly comparing against specifications and calculate the percentage of compliance. The quality review can be applied for scope, customer satisfaction or component deliverables.

Not all projects have equal value in an established portfolio. We need to consider relative strategic benefit when measuring project performance. Project performance measurements will need to consolidated at the Portfolio level.

To measure individual project performance, metrics such as Schedule Performance Index (SPI) and Cost Performance Index (CPI) can be used.

SPI - Schedule Performance Index

The Schedule Performance Index indicates how efficiently you are actually progressing compared to the planned project schedule. The SPI is a measure of schedule efficiency, expressed as the ratio of earned value to planned value. SPI gives you information about the schedule performance of the project. It is the efficiency of the time utilized on the project.

The Schedule Performance Index can be determined by dividing earned value by planned value.

Schedule Performance Index = (Earned Value) / (Planned Value)

SPI = EV / PV

With the above formula, you can conclude that:

- If the SPI is greater than one, this means more work has been completed than the planned work. In other words, you are ahead of schedule.
- If the SPI is less than one, this means less work has been completed than the planned work. In other words, you are behind schedule.
- If the SPI is equal to one, this means work is being completed at about the same rate as planned, you are on time.

Example of the Schedule Performance Index (SPI)

You have a project to be completed in 12 months and the budget of the project is 100,000 USD. Six months have passed and 60,000 USD has been spent, but on closer review, you find that only 40% of the work has been completed so far.

Find the Schedule Performance Index and deduce whether the project is behind or ahead of schedule.

Given in the question:

Actual Cost (AC) = 60,000 USD
Planned Value (PV) = 50% of 100,000 USD
=50,000 USD
Earned Value (EV) = 40% of 100,000 USD
= 40,000 USD
Now,
Schedule Performance Index (SPI) = EV / PV
= 40,000 / 50,000
= 0.8

Hence, the Schedule Performance Index is 0.8

Since the Schedule Performance Index is less than one, you are behind schedule.

CPI - Cost Performance Index

The Cost Performance Index helps you analyze the efficiency of the cost utilized by the project. It measures the value of the work completed compared to the actual cost spent on the project. The Cost Performance Index (CPI) is a measure of the cost efficiency of budgeted resources, expressed as a ratio of earned value to actual cost.

The Cost Performance Index specifies how much you are earning for each dollar spent on the project. The Cost Performance Index is an indication of how well the project is remaining on budget.

Formula for the Cost Performance Index (CPI)

The Cost Performance Index can be determined by dividing earned value by actual cost.

Cost Performance Index = (Earned Value) / (Actual Cost)

CPI = EV / AC

With the above formula, you can conclude that:

- If the CPI is less than one, you are earning less than the amount spent. In other words, you're over budget.
- If the CPI is greater than one, you are earning more than the amount spent. In other words, you are under budget.
- If the CPI is equal to one, this means earning and spending are equal. You can say that you are proceeding exactly as per the planned budget spending, although this rarely happens.

Example of the Cost Performance Index (CPI)

You have a project to be completed in 12 months and the budget of the project is 100,000 USD. Six months have passed and 60,000 USD has been spent, but on closer review, you find that only 40% of the work has been completed so far.

89

The Cost Performance Index for this project will show whether you are under budget or over budget.

Given in the question:

Actual Cost (AC) = 60,000 USD
Planned Value (PV) = 50% of 100,000 USD
= 50,000 USD
Earned Value (EV) = 40% of 100,000 USD
= 40,000 USD
Now,
Cost Performance Index (CPI) = EV / AC
= 40,000 / 60,000
= 0.67

Hence, the Cost Performance Index is 0.67

Since the Cost Performance Index is less than one, this means you are earning 0.67 USD for every 1 USD spent. In other words, you are over budget.

PORTFOLIO METRICS

One method to help decision makers monitor, evaluate, and control portfolio performance against strategic objectives is to use a portfolio dashboard that incorporates benefits. This special dashboard is a simple visual aid to evaluate how the portfolio is performing from a macro perspective, and how the performance of individual projects impacts the strategic objectives they support.

Portfolio Dashboard

The dashboard allows management to focus on troubled projects, where the attention and actions are required.

For example, following on a summary view of portfolio and the status of each project category, it provides the visibility to major changes on high level portfolio as well as individual projects. Keep it simple and stay true to the traffic light concept. It is easy to determine those projects that required actions and where decisions have to be made.

>> *Sample Dashboard Chart 1* <<

>> *Sample Dashboard Chart 2* <<

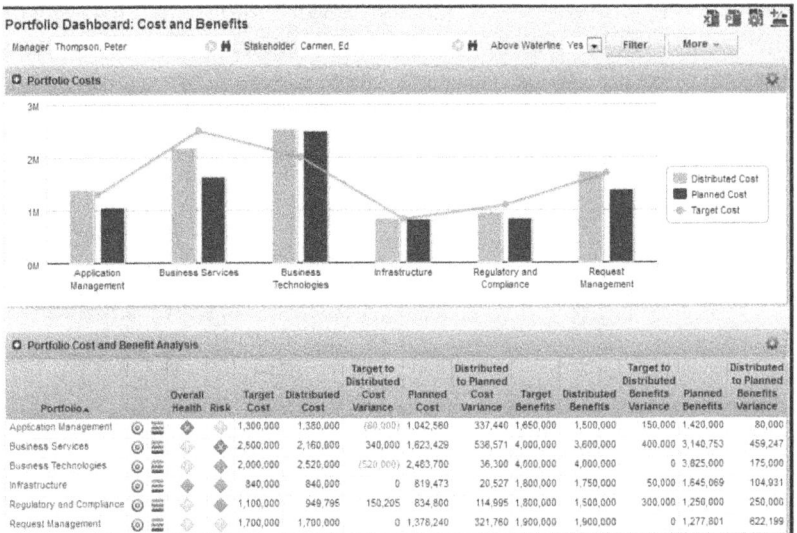

>> *Sample Dashboard Chart 3* <<

There are many commercial tools and solutions on the market. To identify an existing tool best fit to your organization's needs, you may refer to Gartner's recommendation.

Gartner is an American research and advisory firm providing information technology related insight for IT and other business leaders located across the world. Gartner publishes Magic Quadrant each year on general Portfolio Management platforms and solutions.

Portfolio SPI and Portfolio CPI

SPI and CPI from individual projects can be synthesized and consolidated into Portfolio level metrics.

Portfolio SPI is calculated by multiplying each index by its priority of the project, and get the respective Portfolio Index.

For example, Project x's SPI of 1.2 can be multiplied by its priority of 0.2. All projects are calculated using Project SPI multiplied by its priority. The sum is Portfolio SPI.

Portfolio CPI is calculated similarly using Project's CPI value multiplied by its priority and sum them together.

Portfolio Benefits Metrics

Portfolio Benefits Metrics addresses how portfolio performance can be assessed in terms of achieving strategic goals and objectives.

It is important to assess current portfolio performance with respect to continued expectation of achieving strategic objectives as projects move through execution. It is not guaranteed that the **Expected Benefits** will remain static as the portfolio moves through implementation.

The **Planned Benefits** represent the weighted priorities of all candidate projects with respect to one another. The **Planned Benefits** usually do not change until a reprioritization is performed in the strategic plan.

With the consideration of project risks, the **Planned Benefits** will be reduced by resulting **Expected Benefits**. Usually, the optimal portfolio represents the combination of projects with the highest total **Expected Benefits**, rather than the highest total **Planned Benefits** under specified potential threats.

As project and portfolio execution proceed, risks are encountered and managed. Risks can affect Expected Benefits by increasing or decreasing the likelihood of success of delivering organization's goals and objectives

Risk that is described in earlier section, is a metric closely related to achieving project and portfolio benefit.

Risk represents the likelihood that a project will not complete successfully.

If the project does not complete successfully, it will not deliver its Planned Benefits as originally anticipated. It will not subsequently help the organization to achieve its strategic objectives.

Risk can be used to assess changes in the Expected Benefits values that originally resulted in selection of the project for the portfolio.

Risk can be used for each reporting period to measure and discount Planned Benefits to produce a current Expected Benefits for the reporting period.

As projects and portfolios are implemented and work progresses, we can monitor and forecast the likelihood of delivering strategic benefits after completion. Over time, variance in Expected Benefits comparing to Planned Benefits can be used to define how well the projects remain on track to deliver the strategic benefits.

Project Expected Benefits and the **Portfolio Expected Benefits** can help evaluate projects and portfolios against **Planned Benefits**. Project risk will change after project portfolio selection and as project work progresses. Comparing current project and portfolio **Expected Benefits** to **Planned Benefits** can help operations portfolio management evaluate the portfolio's progress in delivering strategic objectives.

Portfolio Performance information can be combined to produce portfolio performance measurements that reflect strategic benefit.

Portfolio Benefits Metrics are tools to synthesize individual project performance measurements and relative strategic benefits. This produces the strategic portfolio level performance metrics. Now it is possible to leverage OPM Tools to visually illustrate them in a dashboard. Management can make proactive decisions about necessary adjustment of projects within the portfolio, or the portfolio as a whole.

Strategic Alignment Metrics

- The number of projects – and the percentage of total money invested in each – related to each business objective
- The number of strategic projects delivered versus the total number of strategic projects
- Return on investment, broken down by program and portfolio and investment
- % of Portfolio spend in run the business
- % of Portfolio in grow the business
- % of Portfolio in innovate the business
- % of Portfolio in Short/Medium/Long-term projects
- % of portfolio in Large and Extra Large Projects

Demand & Capacity Metrics

Do we have the right prioritization and sequencing of projects given current capacity?

- % of growth in project request pipeline
- % of growth in prioritized Initiatives
- Resource utilization (human, material, capital)
- Recruiting pipeline
- Supply and Pipeline turnaround time/Capacity

Operational Efficiency Metrics

- Percentage of projects in each portfolio that have been delivered on time/budget based on the total number of projects within the portfolio
- Time to market, or time from idea creation to market, broken into the length of each phase of the process

- Resource usage numbers in relation to budgeted amounts
- The percentage of effort, broken down by time spent working on projects versus maintenance
- Number of completed projects versus canceled or on-hold projects
- Dollar saved on consolidation efforts

Execution Metrics

- Failure and success rates of projects delivered on time/budget
- Budget deviation, or actual cost versus planned cost per project
- Project quality metrics – number of defects, time to close defects
- Number of change requests/enhancements per project
- Resource utilization by each phase in project – actual versus budgeted
- Risk Management – number of identified risks and mitigation plan
- Dollars Committed but not spent

Value Delivered Metrics

- Benefits realization against benefits forecast
- Customer or user satisfaction percentage – change in percentage compared to prior period
- Cost savings or increased revenue
- Increased productivity
- Minimized or elimination of risks

OPERATIONS PORTFOLIO MANAGEMENT TOOLS

Many organizations use Excel Spreadsheets to manage Operations Portfolio Management activities, and they are good for managing organizational activities. Templates are defined, macros and formulas are utilized to make the operation more efficient. There are also graphs and charts to visualize the status.

There are also many specific tools supporting a variety of Operations Portfolio Management activities including Microsoft Project, SmartSheet Cloud Solutions.

There are also Gartner reports on Magic Quadrant for Portfolio Management. Providers in this Magic Quadrant include those focused on general-purpose or enterprise wide Portfolio Management. For example, Planview, Changepoint, CA Technologies and many others are used for many enterprise companies.

When evaluating and positioning the vendors included in this research, emphasis is placed on the importance of vendors offering multiple Portfolio Management products supporting different use cases including Enterprise-wide Portfolio Management, Reporting Portfolio Management, Collaborative Portfolio Mangement and Internal IT Portfolio Management.

Personally, I prefer and frequently use the following tools. I find them to be very easy to use, with very low maintenance cost. Also, they easily support collaboration among many people,

- SmartSheet
- ServiceNow
- Google Sheets

WHO ARE THE BIG PLAYERS IN OPM?

The major players in the Global consulting market are the firms that are collectively referred to as the Big 5.

These firms are:

- Accenture (formerly Andersen Consulting)
- Deloitte Touche Consulting (Deloitte Consulting)
- Ernst & Young
- KPMG Consulting
- PriceWaterhouseCoopers

Each Big 5 firm sets top-tier standards for excellence and capability in the delivery of business consulting services, including Portfolio Management. The breadth and depth of expertise across all professional disciplines is truly impressive.

Strategy consultants are having to transform themselves and the way they work in response to changing client demands, and the impact of digital technology on businesses. These big players have the ability to deliver a packaged end-to-end solution for clients including Portfolio Analysis, Risk Assessment and Process Reengineering.

REAL WORLD CASE STUDY – STARTUP COMPANY

Startup companies often handle many risks that are no less than those being handled by larger business. It is very important to accurately assess **Risk** across the entire startup business portfolio.

Several years ago, I started a technical consulting company that deploys and supports customers' enterprise system solutions.

Strategize

When a business gets started, we usually have an overall idea of what we need to do, although not everything is very clear at the beginning. We spent a lot of time setting strategies.

For example, we asked ourselves:

- Who is our customer
- What service/products are we providing
- How will we provide value for our customers
- What strategies will we employ to grow the business
- And finally, how will we generate profit

Along with those discussions and brainstorming, we decided that our startup business will focus on medium size growing companies, between small and big cap companies.

The reason is that big companies are pretty mature and fully established. Big companies already have their vendor base so it's not easy to penetrate. On the other hand, for smaller business, they just get started and they have a lot of things to do. However, they are also tight on budget and their business may not be stable.

We focused on those medium size growing companies because, in addition to being in growth mode, they also have a stronger need to get their operations stabilized. Also, they have the desire and financial strengths.

We believed this was an opportunity for us to focus. Once we have that in mind, it really helped and aligned us at a strategy level. This enabled us to focus our limited resource and money to establish our business engagement model.

Prioritize

After we aligned on strategy, the next step is to prioritize all those different activities. We can do many things like providing enterprise services, helping companies to developing their solutions, and/or we can develop our own product. There are many different ways to run a startup. We had to prioritize and focus on limited items we can do.

We determined that with all those opportunities and activities, we would start with enterprise service delivery. In other words, we will help our clients design, implement and support their solutions for their business needs.

Also, we were doing the initial in-house product designs in parallel. We can afford to do initial design and proof of concept without necessarily burning a lot of the money.

After six months, as the revenue comes in from our clients, we are able to utilize the revenue we received, and allocate it to fund our future product development.

Prioritization is very important because we can certainly do a lot of things, but due to the limited resource and money, we have to prioritize. We have to determine what are the most important things.

In our situation, we decided to focus on service delivery first, and then, after we achieved initial goal, we would review our priorities, and made necessary adjustments. Actually, this worked out pretty well.

Optimize

Once we had a strategy and knew our priority, the next step is operations, focusing on delivery. It is quite important to manage our available resources and learn to handle dependencies in different areas.

For example, we only had a handful of key resources. We managed them very carefully and ensured those people are properly assigned being utilized effectively. We had to keep the balance.

On one side we want them to be fully utilized. On the other side, we don't want to over-utilize them. Otherwise, they will get burned out very quickly. We just want to make sure it's a sustainable model to manage those key resources. In those early days, we used simple spreadsheet to track their projects, tasks and estimated duration and hours.

Regarding money, we had limited funding. We are very careful to manage the cashflow. When we provided the service delivery, the money didn't come in right away.

Quite often, we had to wait for a couple months in order to see the money being paid to us. When we run the financial spending forecast, we have to understand the revenue will come in at later stages, while we have to pay for service resource cost upfront. We had to optimize our billing cycle and send out invoices to clients as quickly as we could, and it helped the financial operations tremendously.

Another example of optimizing our key resources was using the different resource mix during the whole delivery cycle. During the initial engagement and design, we assigned our most experienced senior resources to understand requirements, and design solutions. During service delivery, we leveraged our global resources on the implementation. On the financial side, we negotiated terms with our partners so that we don't have to pay them upfront because they agreed to wait until we got paid from our clients.

Track

We do micro monitor, but not micro manage. When we empowered our managers and our technical staff, and trust them, they can do a really good job. At the same time, we put measurements and metrics in place. For example, for the business development, we must know the number of business leads we have, the number of follow-ups we are doing, response rate, conversion rate weekly, and how effective marketing and promotion efforts are.

Regarding service deliver and resource management, we needed to understand how many hours out consultants are working weekly and whether we are properly managing their timesheet. Also, we have to submit invoice to our clients consistently. If we did not get paid on time, we would know immediately and we can track them down in a very timely manner.

From business operational perspective, visibility on operational details is very important. We can't assume everything works fine; we have to monitor the overall operations very, very closely.

Startup companies are full of excitement and dynamics. At the same time business can change very quickly. It is very beneficial to put the OPM structure in place in anticipating that things are going to be different, things are going to be changing.

We must have the OPM help manage those business dynamics so that we can stay focused when things are changing. OPM enables us to:

- respond, react, and adjust our priorities
- staying focused on the business goals
- help us understand our constraints and our competitions.

The bottom line: When we adopt Operational Portfolio Management, it help the business to run smoothly in a very organized and structure way.

Risk Management

For many startup companies, one area commonly overlooked is Risk Management. The mentality is, "Okay, I knew the risk, but I am too busy. We will deal with it as it occurs."

Unfortunately, if we don't pay enough attention, it may potentially kill the company when it does happen. So we have to be mindful, understand how risk management would work and put something in place as it will really, really help the company when those risks do happen, as we know how to deal with them.

When managing a startup, we have to deal with many risks such as Financial Risks, Operational Risks as well as Strategic Risks.

Financial risk

Critical to long-term success, this includes things such as funding risk, investment risk, pricing risk, or credit risk.

Regarding costs, any increase in expenditure is a pressure for startups, since they are often operating on a tight budget. Labor costs, fuel costs, marketing campaign costs in a competitive environment, etc., can dry up company's budget quickly. Many startup companies do not possess a sufficient cash flow but rather rely heavily on ongoing operations to generate funds for the continuous activities.

We had to manage the company's cashflow very carefully. Usually, we had to pay our consultants before we received any payments from our customers. Keeping sufficient cash reserve is very critical.

Also, we need to track and provide invoices to our customers on a very timely manner. In addition, we asked our account managers to focus on collecting customer payments (Key Accounts Receivable) and timesheet management (Key Accounts Payable) very closely.

The consequences an organization may suffer from financial risks varies with the scale of the company's financial transactions. For example, the borrowed funds must be balanced in comparison to its business scope. The cashflow is relative low when we manage 1 or 2 projects. The financial transactions were significantly bigger when we manage a dozen or more projects. The pressure and risk for cashflow is much more intense for 12 concurrent projects compared with conducting just 2 projects.

There was a situation where the need for funds was not well planned and cash generation did not meet our cash flow forecast. Our business ran low on cash, and we were forced to postpone upcoming projects. As we learned the lesson, we established business line of credit as a method for reducing risks.

We also changed our financial fiscal year to be ending on March 30th. This helped us avoid year-end financial chaos compared to a fiscal year ending December 31.

When it comes to budget, every penny counts for many startups. Even though larger corporations are not always in better position with resources, they have many more options to allocate resources than the capability of startups. Startups are regarded as open to risk taking, and this is why top leaders in a startup should stay focused on risk management.

Operational risks

These frequently are summarized as human risks: human error leads to business operations failure.

Nevertheless, operational risks include all risks that arise from the organization's internal activities involving people, products or services offered, operational systems, and external factors. A high degree of employee turnover and/or a shortage of know-how experts both result in wastage of manpower and additional cost of training. In the long term, the human factor will raise or lower operational productivity and affect the brand image of startup as an employer.

For example, during our internal timesheet review, we identified a consultant who billed excessive hours and unauthorized expense items to our customer. Although we trust our people, we have to have an internal system to validate and verify.

Small day-to-day losses due to customer dissatisfaction or bad reputation can add up and cost any company significant damage financially as well as market performance. A crucial step in managing operational risk is to monitor, review and update current management data and structure.

Compared to businesses in other industries, high-tech companies have a stronger capacity for innovation, higher technology efficiency and, consequently, higher exposure to technology related risks.

Risks in companies providing technology products or services particularly involve intellectual property, asset and system issues. While technology requires its own innovative operation systems, the need to manage those systems are equally essential. Key innovations are the soul of technology companies' operations. Leakage of confidential information will lead to violation of copyright from competitors or from customers; reputation damage and market losses.

If you are managing a technology consulting company, it is strongly recommended to patent, trademark or register your inventions and products. Proper maintenance of technology output includes confidentiality agreements with employees and customers to avoid business materials and intellectual property being stolen and/or leaked out.

Strategic risks

These are the probabilities of a loss arising from a poor strategic business plan, decision, or from the inconsistent and inappropriate implementation according to the plan.

Strategic risks pose a threat to earnings, capital availability and corporation's viability. Strategic plans indicate the operation direction as well as framework, vision and objectives of an organization. The lower the probability of strategic risk stays on a consistent basis, the stronger the organization is and will remain.

We engaged with Corporate Accounting very closely since that function focuses on business accounting and maintaining an organization's financial records. It ensures compliancy with laws, regulations and the organization's policies, as well as providing the information executives need to make the right financial decisions for the organization.

Another important area to focus on is legal compliance and protection. Corporate and commercial lawyers are experts in company and business law. They understand the differences between legal entities and how to best utilize them for different purposes. They also assist companies in various transactions supporting business operations.

Senior management constantly needs to balance the priority between growth and profit margin. It is quite common to set the focus on growth in this current quarter, and shift the priority to profit margin next quarter. For startups, it is quite common to constantly adjust priorities based on dynamic and competitive business environment.

Board of directors focus on how organizations identify, assess and manage company's risks. Strategic risk management requires concentrations on risks to shareholder value as the ultimate goal while considering the effect of external and internal scenarios to the ability of organization to achieve its goals.

In my experiences, a board of directors have following three very important roles.

(1) Establish competent executive team

The board needs to identify right management talents to supplement existing executive team. It helps strengthen the weakness of the management team and fill critical management vacancy.

For example, the board must bring strong and capable executive to lead Sales and Marketing operations if the existing management team is strong on product design and weak on sales.

Although It is not an easy process, we worked with our executive recruiter so that he understood our requirements and expectations. During the candidate selection and evaluation process, we focused on their relevant experiences and measurable accomplishments. Generally, we did not focus too much on what's written on candidates' resume. Instead, we discuss about candidates' experiences and his thinking and approach on delivering our strategic objectives in sales.

(2) Mitigate Business Risks

The board must understand potential business risks and provide continuity of an organization's delivery on strategy.

Risk management issues have been at an all-time high. Boards can continue to expect risk management to be an increasingly challenging part of board decision-making.

Board members must have a good understanding of risk management, even when they lack expertise in that area. Boards may ask for the expertise of outside consultants to help them review organization's risks when they lack expertise in that area.

It is helpful to familiarize the management team with expectations within the industry or regulatory bodies that the organization operates.

Of all the risk management challenges that boards face, the greatest challenge is in navigating organizational growth while protecting the organization from unnecessary risk, so that it doesn't impact the business negatively.

For example, the board must ask executives, managers and employees are compliant with laws and policies in all areas.

(3) Enforce fiscal accountability.

The board needs to monitor the actual performance against the budget. The board needs to monitor organization's cashflow as it has duty to avoid becoming insolvent. In addition to an annual budget, a longer term strategy can build organization's financial strength.

The board ensures there are financial resources. This may include seeking additional venture capital investment, individual investment or business line of credit.

Business Insurance

It is a fact that risks can be managed and controlled but not totally eliminated. Thus even with the most thoroughly planned, evaluated and implemented risk management plan, errors can unexpectedly arise at some point of the process. One of the risk management techniques is risk transfer, which involves insurance. Insurance is one solution of organizations to hedge against threats.

For example, the company has to consider a number of insurance policies, such as Property, General Liability, Worker's compensation and Commercial Auto.

To be insurable, the risks should appear to match several common characteristics. For example, insurers normally agree to:

1. contract homogeneous risks,
2. contract risks that historically have large number of similar events, and
3. ensure the claim costs.

Insurable risks need not to be categorized as catastrophic but have definite loss when measured within particular time and amount. This means the impact of risk is measurable, and the benefit of the insurance can be determined.

Doing business means being liable to risks, from slightly to heavily. However, it is not worth insuring against all uncertainties and risks.

Summary

Generally, startups in an expanding stage reckon themselves as a risk. Thus, startups regularly confront risks offensively to grow, while larger firms take risk defensively, to ensure the operation strength.

In a startup work environment where every activity is wholly involved, each directly affects the other. Risk management in a startup business should not be an individual program but integrate with other management processes: business strategy planning, human resources management, financial management, and customer relationship management.

By their nature, startups are frequently found by entrepreneurs-- successful and optimistic entrepreneurs. These leaders have the tendency to be confident based on their success in establishing and leading the business, resulting in many startups putting risk management plans far down the list of priorities.

Risk management is vital in securing the business' capitals and other properties. However, risk accompanies the business' opportunities to grow.

Therefore, it is often emphasized in business strategies that risk management is not to prohibit taking risks entirely, but to understand the levels of risks, and to properly engage risks into development and growth.

Risk management emphasizes the capabilities of a business to anticipate changes, not the avoid risk. Avoidance of risks means waiting for the event to happen then react to it, rather than prepare for the changes.

Here are my thoughts on startups as a conclusion,

Many of original concepts don't translate when we were running at early stage of a startup. Many entrepreneurs run business operations on gut instinct, play things up near the wire, and have difficulties to focus.

I realize that what works well when we complete a proof of concept does not necessary ensure the final success when we go to the final production.

Ad-hoc decisions and random good luck are not the secret recipe. Instead, it is discipline, preparation and calculated risk taking, backed by solid understanding of your target market and its real needs.

REAL WORLD CASE STUDY – LARGE GLOBAL ORGANIZATION

The company, one of the largest hi-tech manufacturers in the world, had acquired two multi-billion-dollar companies, and now found itself at a crossroads. Having spent significant time creating a good strategic plan for the company, it was essential to now improve execution and delivery.

Executive leadership recognized the effectiveness of aligning projects and strategy, and realized that the company now had three different set of project management processes. They were ad hoc and inconsistent across various enterprise projects.

The company had begun the process of building a centralized Enterprise Project Management Office (PMO). The PMO organization would need energy, support, and sponsorship if it were going to achieve the highest potential value that an PMO could deliver.

The PMO had to first go through an evaluation step to understand the existing structure and process from three existing companies including the main company, and two companies being acquired. The second step was confirming the structure and processes to be deployed for all 3 companies.

As a result of those evaluations, the company identified four key challenges with respect to PMO and associated strategic capabilities:

- Clearly defining pragmatic scope, objectives, and role expectations for the PMO
- Enabling effective delivery of large projects
- Developing organizational capability in project management methods
- Providing executive level education to effectively support project management methods.

Some of the solutions agreed upon included:

110

- Developed a roadmap for PMO formation, while coaching and mentoring the PMO team to drive ongoing results.

- Conduct Discovery, a process of stakeholder interviews and process mapping to identify gaps and develop a roadmap to drive subsequent capability improvement.

- Review and Align with executives, get their support and sponsorship

- Define details of process, Roles &Responsibilities including templates and examples, utilize online tools for efficiency

- Refine the process with direct feedback and suggestions

- Retain dedicated resource focusing the roll out and ongoing operations

- Initiate capability improvement efforts based on the roadmap. Where practical, capability improvements were initiated in parallel with roadmap completion.

- Create the momentum that set the organization on a course for cultural change.

- Schedule Kick-off sessions and following up with training

During the Kick-off session, the following items were communicated, discussed and aligned,

- Team Structure and Governance
- Background and Overview
- Objectives & Strategic Goals
- Success Factors and Criteria
- Issues, Risks, and Assumptions
- High-level Milestones
- High-level Communications Plan
- Change Management Plan

Executives agreed that the No. 1 priority was doing the right projects, so strategic alignment was a first step. The PMO identifies the portfolio and classify projects, developing a clear list of active and pending projects and a portfolio process that spelled out how to intake new projects, prioritize, and manage the portfolio.

The Company was determined to empower and develop a team and make them an integral part of the transformation process. An PMO organizational structure was established, along with role and responsibility definitions and a management framework.

In alignment with their corporate values, project management and project portfolio management methodologies were developed, and workshops on the methodology delivered throughout the organization.

These efforts were successful, and as a result, the combined company standardized the portfolio framework and delivery methodology across the enterprise.

- All enterprise projects use standard portfolio management process to get registered, prioritized, funded and managed, allowing the company to have a clear view of all enterprise initiatives and their investment decisions.

- Guided the enterprise-wide development of a project management culture, a significant organizational change.

- Stronger partnership between project teams and business leaders, and transparency of Project Inventory and Status.

- Prioritization of project selection and timing including the declination of projects that did not meet strategic objectives.

Compared to small companies, big companies have larger organizations, often with employees around the world. One very important thing is alignment. It is always a challenge to keep everyone in big organization on the same page on corporate vision and objectives. It is a constant effort to ensure we are all clear on what we want to achieve, what we need to do, and our priorities.

Establishing Operations Portfolio Management governance enabled us to have full alignment, and have standard metrics to measure the overall performance.

After Strategizing and Prioritization, key activities and initiatives at organization level becomes critical. For many big organizations, it's common that there are many projects being conducted in silos among different functions. People managing those projects may not necessarily talk to each other if the governance is not there, or not effective. Therefore, this is an important step to evaluate and prioritize all key enterprise activities, cross enterprise, cross organization, and cross the whole company.

When we go through the prioritization process, we have to keep a balance. There are some short term tactical projects that we cannot postpone and have to do, and also there are some long-term strategic initiatives we have to get started. With these long term initiatives, it takes time to see the return, but we have to prioritize them and get them started. Also, delivering on strategies must be our primary focus.

For large companies where there are always a lot of things happening, it is very easy to get defocused. Regardless of what is happening, we always need to focus on what's the most important thing for the entire organization during the prioritization process.

Another important aspect is Optimization. As the company is quite big, initiatives tend to involve many people, many resources, and many vendors. When we get process and activities organized and structured, it's a lot easier for everyone to have the same visibility. With better visibility, we can manage our key resources more effectively and increase their utilization. These resources can potentially perform more efficiently with better results.

During Optimization, another factor to be considered is cross-functional dependency. For example, project, A is on very high priority, but it cannot start until project B is completed. So, project A is dependent on the completion of project B. In this case, we need to rearrange key resources from project A until project B is done.

As part of Optimization, we can constantly realign our resources for better utilization.

There are many moving pieces and puzzles to be sorted out within OPM. Keeping transparency and consistency is always highly recommended. At the Corporate organization level, we must keep track the overall progress. We need to ensure all key activities like projects and services, are delivered based on our desired business objectives.

Another important item is enforcing management control. We don't want to Micro Manage, but we do Micro Monitor. This means management can always intervene whenever it is necessary.

FINAL THOUGHTS

The organization needs to transfer cutting edge research into strategies. Operations Portfolio Management enforces an organization's planning processes.

To achieve organizations strategic goals, we have to ask ourselves whether we have a good understanding of all risks, and whether we have a careful risk controls.

Operations Portfolio Management brings rationality in the allocation of resources, including human, equipment and financial.

For some companies, the scarcest resource is not money but people. A critical factor in project selection is resource availability.

- Can we afford to add a new service with our existing resource capacity?
- Do we have a qualified PM who can manage this project?
- Do we have all critical resources available for this project?

Operations Portfolio Management brings visibility to project progress, service level and people utilization.

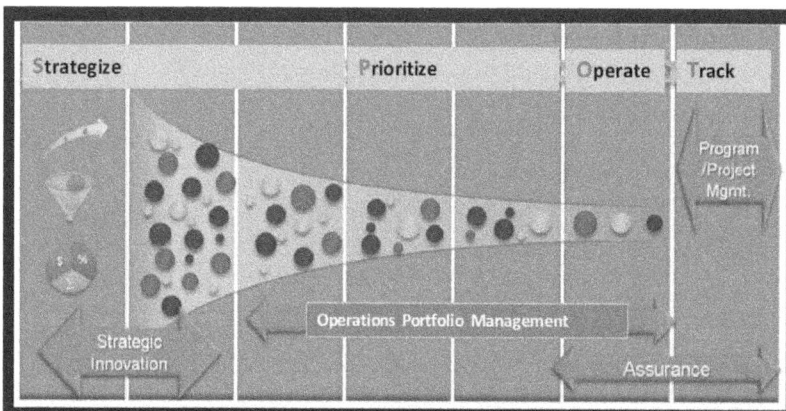

>> SPOT OPM Diagram <<.